Choosing Home

of related interest

Homeschooling the Child with Asperger Syndrome
Real Help for Parents Anywhere and On Any Budget
Lise Pyles
ISBN 1 84310 461 9

Home Educating Our Autistic Spectrum Children
Paths are Made by Walking
Edited by Terri Dowty and Kitt Cowlishaw
ISBN 1 84310 037 1

Parenting a Child with Asperger Syndrome
200 Tips and Strategies
Brenda Boyd
ISBN 1 84310 137 8

Freaks, Geeks and Asperger Syndrome
A User Guide to Adolescence
Luke Jackson
ISBN 1 84310 098 3

Getting Services for Your Child on the Autism Spectrum
DeAnn Hyatt-Foley and Matthew G. Foley
ISBN 1 85302 991 2

Pretending to be Normal
Living with Asperger's Syndrome
Liane Holliday Willey
ISBN 1 85302 749 9

Aspergers Syndrome
A Guide for Parents and Professionals
Tony Attwood
ISBN 1 85302 577 1

Choosing Home

Deciding to Homeschool
with Asperger's Syndrome

Martha Kennedy Hartnett

Foreword by Stephen Shore

Jessica Kingsley Publishers
London and New York

First published in the United Kingdom in 2004
by Jessica Kingsley Publishers Ltd
116 Pentonville Road
London N1 9JB, England
and
29 West 35th Street, 10th fl.
New York, NY 10001-2299, USA

www.jkp.com

Copyright © Martha Kennedy Hartnett 2004
Foreword copyright © Stephen Shore 2004

Library of Congress Cataloging in Publication Data
A CIP catalog record for this book is available from the Library of Congress

British Library Cataloguing in Publication Data
A CIP catalogue record for this book is available from the British Library

ISBN 1 84310 763 5

Printed and Bound in Great Britain by
Athenaeum Press, Gateshead, Tyne and Wear

For Anthony and Patrick
Thank you for sharing
the Asperger's journey with me

Contents

Foreword

Choosing Home: Deciding to Homeschool with Asperger's Syndrome is about the incredible courage and determination exhibited by James along with his parents as they strive to provide a meaningful education for their son. The story you are about to read makes an important and substantial contribution to the education of people with Asperger's Syndrome. Right from the first page of the preface Martha displays a rare talent for bringing the reader into the world of the child with Asperger's Syndrome and his family in their successful struggles to create an educational environment where "there are no learning disabilities." Through the lives of James and his parents Celia and John, the reader learns of the real-life stresses, trials, and tribulations that take place when the school environment goes wrong as well as the successes that can be had when it is made right.

James and his family were able to hold their lives together during the elementary school days – sort of. While able to "demonstrate good social skills" in school, James would erupt like a volcano from pent up frustration, anger, and tension once he entered his mother's car for the drive home. With the stresses of school rippling through the entire family like a tsunami, it became clear that home schooling was necessary by middle school. Ever conscientious and desiring to work with the school system, Celia and John developed a plan with the superintendent to satisfy most of the educational requirements at home while attending to socialization goals at school. Trapped in an atmosphere of intolerance, bullying and sensory violations in the middle school, this strategy failed miserably.

Shortly thereafter, John realized that he was desperately providing support from the fringe of a negative education situation and, with a dramatic shift to active involvement in his son's education, advocated for pulling James from public school completely. From James' euphoria at being told of his withdrawal from his torture at school to his "thank you for homeschooling me," it becomes clear that full homeschooling was the right thing to do. Instead of the social isolation feared by the superintendent occurring, James' homeschooling laid the groundwork for a life of independence and self-determination. Empowered to provide input into designing his own curriculum along with tutors who cater to his interests and strengths, James flourishes in this new educational environment. Homeschooling saved his life.

As discussed by Martha, socialization for many children with Asperger's Syndrome is not learning about getting along with others, but rather a negativity endurance test. The homeschooling environment provided James with the temporal, cognitive, and emotional space to learn socialization on a more realistic incidental basis in his community. As the reader will find, James learned well, but needed academic and socialization experiences provided for him in ways that he could process in manageable doses.

An especially strong point of *Choosing Home* is that in addition to basking the reader in the sheen of James' success, Martha insightfully describes the process of hard work, determination, and sheer courage to stand up for what is right even in the face of adversity. *Choosing Home* is also a wonderful guide and resource chock-full of suggestions on developing curriculum to make education "learning disability-free," networking with the large community of other parents involved in homeschooling, engaging child input, developing material for "off" days, and keeping a journal to help deal with the inevitable challenges that arise from homeschooling.

As *Choosing Home* draws to a close Martha takes a hard look at the realities of homeschooling ranging from needing to keep a realistic outlook to respecting boundaries, and serving more as a facilitator than a didactic teacher. Finally, she drives home the point that preventing potential burnout and caring for oneself are vital toward enabling one to take care of others.

I highly recommend this book to anyone interested in homeschooling as well as to people wanting to know more about the challenges surrounding Asperger's Syndrome, the family, and education. Educating a child at home is not for everyone, but for those in need, it can be a lifesaver.

Stephen Shore, August 2003
Brookline, Massachusetts
Author of Beyond the Wall: Personal Experiences with Autism and Asperger Syndrome

What is Asperger's Syndrome?

Asperger's Syndrome is a recently defined, neurodevelopmental condition which has sometimes been called "mild or high functioning autism." It has been included in the DSM IV category of Pervasive Developmental Disorders (PDD), a very broad and somewhat controversial term used to describe individuals who have 1. restricted, repetitive, and stereotyped patterns of behavior, 2. defects in communication skills, and 3. significant difficulties in reciprocal, social interactions. Increasingly, PDD is being conceptualized as a continuum running from the most severe form of autism (i.e., Autistic Disorder) through varying degrees of severity which extend to the high functioning edge of the spectrum where AS is located. While individuals with AS retain certain characteristics of more severe autism, AS is characterized by cognitive functioning which falls in the normal or above average range and by generally normal language functioning, although there are a range of subtle, but significant abnormalities of pragmatic language invariably present.

Specifically, some characteristics which result in the social dysfunction of Asperger's Syndrome may include the following: 1. inability to read non-verbal cues and facial expressions of others, 2. poor eye contact, and 3. awkward body language. These characteristics contribute to poor understanding of social experience.

Paradoxically, while individuals with Asperger's are sometimes brilliant in specific areas of their interest, they are often concrete in their thinking, particularly about real life situations. Executive functioning, i.e. understanding how details relate to each other and to a main point can be difficult for them. Fluid reasoning or problem-solving can also be hard. "Getting the big picture," understanding the intention of others, or shifting point of view are major difficulties. Cognitive flexibility is impaired as is ability to shift sets and take a new perspective. Generalizability from one situation to another is also problematic.

Often right-hemispheric insufficiency is present, characterized by non-verbal learning disabilities, difficulties with transitions and novel, unpredicted experience, and new situations. Indeed, difficulty with neurointegration, a problem with integrating complex visual experience, is central to the disorder and is exhibited in visual-spatial and visual motor problems present in psychological testing and in life experience. Motor clumsiness, tactile defensiveness, and hypersensitivity to light or sound are also often present.

It should be noted that individuals at this highest end of the autistic spectrum present very differently from each other. Often, they exhibit only some of the most overt characteristics described. Some individuals have more erratic and challenging behaviors in early childhood, but have moved up the spectrum as they mature. Consequently, a thorough early history of an individual is an important part of the diagnostic evaluation for Asperger's. There is often comorbidity with Attention Deficit Hyperactivity Disorder (ADHD), Obsessive Compulsive Disorder (OCD), non-verbal learning disabilities and depression.

Since its inclusion in DSM IV, AS has lately been diagnosed with such increasing frequency that today many child psychiatrists and educators are alluding to an "epidemic," probably caused by better case finding, correction of prior misdiagnosis, and possibly, over-diagnosis. A positive outcome of greater publicity about the disorder is that individuals with Asperger's Syndrome are more likely now to receive special supports at school, home, and work. At school, such supports can include a special one-to-one aide through the school day, modifications in homework, special tutoring, occupational therapy, physical therapy, adaptive physical education, pragmatic speech therapy, and social skills groups.

Programming for adults, such as modifications in the work setting, is just beginning as awareness of the disorder increases. With support, adults with Asperger's have found employment in structured, predictable fields that utilize their strengths. Some adults seek more repetitious, narrow employment in areas requiring minimal social encounters. Some adults marry and have children, while others live with family or independently as adults. While accommodations for the social limitations of adults with Asperger's are often necessary, with support, these individuals can find friendship and satisfaction in adult life. Organizations dedicated to providing contact and educational information about Asperger's Syndrome have sprung up on the local, national and international levels, providing additional assistance for adults with Asperger's Syndrome to access others with the disorder and available resources.

Daniel W. Rosenn, MD
Barbara H. Rosenn, Psy.D.

Daniel Rosenn, MD is a general and child psychiatrist in Wellesley, MA, specializing in Asperger's Syndrome. **Barbara H. Rosenn**, Psy.D. is a psychologist in Wellesley, MA, who works with adults with Asperger's Syndrome. Both are on the Board of Directors of the Asperger's Association of New England.

Preface

The purpose of this book is to bring an important message to the families of children with Asperger's Syndrome (AS). The message is that homeschooling is an effective educational option available to them. Many parents with Asperger's children have found that, by utilizing homeschooling, their children's lives (and their own) have become happier and learning takes place with greater success.

As they watch their child's self-image and confidence improve, parents find that the stresses of dealing with the school system no longer dominate their own lives. In the world of homeschooling there are no learning disabilities. You simply do what needs to be done for your child to learn in a comfortable and stress-free environment – his own home.

Homeschooling is definitely not for everyone. It often means a change in lifestyle and parental burnout is always looming. If managed well, however, home education can be a vehicle for greater learning and better social development. It offers an opportunity for you and your Asperger's child to share a wonderful world of knowledge and love.

Most people reading this book will be the parents or caregivers of children who have already received a diagnosis of AS. Whatever your contact with AS, remember that it is the unique people in the world who often contribute the most to it. This world needs those who see it through different eyes. They force the rest of us to question ourselves, the way we think and the path on which we may be walking. They cause those who often blindly follow the masses to pause and, in doing so, become more enlightened.

CHAPTER ONE

Struggling

There is no doubt that many young people with AS struggle in today's schools. Their daily academic, emotional, and social ordeals are often painful to witness. Each day brings experiences which, through the lens of Asperger's, can become magnified into trauma. In an effort to help their child, eliminate stress and find a sense of family balance, many parents of AS children are turning to home education. Occasionally this life-altering decision is made with the encouragement of teachers who truly care about what is best for the Asperger's student. Whether such support is present or not, learning at home is growing in popularity as a legal and effective educational alternative.

Families who have chosen to center education around the security of home report benefits to the Asperger's child that are worth consideration. Such benefits include greater levels of self-esteem and responsibility, more time for learning self-help skills, and a contagious enthusiasm for learning. As the pressures associated with school interactions fall away, parents are able to see the AS child with new appreciation. More importantly, the student can learn at his own pace in a respectful environment.

Signals that all is not well at school are often overlooked as parents worry about opportunities for socialization and special education needs. The rewards are great for those who notice the signals and are brave enough to trust their own abilities to educate and guide the Asperger's child. Making the actual decision to choose home for education has been the most difficult step for families who long to take control over their lives. The story of James and his mother, Celia, reveals the process of making such a decision. The results of their choice are inspiring. Although their situation reached a crescendo during the middle school years, families can be drawn to homeschool at any grade level.

James' early grades were spent at a local elementary school where the staff made serious attempts to accommodate his needs. Celia's recollections of this time provide sharp contrast to her son's later educational experiences.

> My son received an early diagnosis of PDD-NOS.[1] Alert special education teachers at his school stumbled across a paper on Hyperlexia and thought it seemed to fit James. They brought it to my attention. My husband and I were able to independently obtain this accurate diagnosis for our son when he was eight. As his preoccupation with reading lessened, the diagnosis was changed to

Asperger's Syndrome. James tested in the superior IQ range and was extremely talented in art.

James was placed with capable teachers who worked hard to implement an IEP (Individualized Educational Plan) my husband and I were comfortable with. An effort was made throughout the school community to highlight James' art talents. This was used as a way to bring him positive attention and direct focus away from the social and sensory difficulties he had at school. There were trying days when James was overwhelmed by the environment around him. He was a very bright, gentle boy but he struggled with a literal interpretation of language, social miscues and an obvious lack of empathy for his classmates. Trouble always surfaced during recess, lunch or any time there was little imposed structure. Any unexpected change of routine was also a potential problem.

My husband and I brainstormed with the special education team to deal with these trouble spots and for the most part were able to make the days manageable for our son. He was fortunate to have a speech and language pathologist who worked hand in hand with us to implement workable strategies. As the strategies worked, he grew more confident. His third grade teacher became a great advocate and friend. To this day she is still one of James' dearest friends.

The key to success was a system of communication developed between the teachers and myself where we would let each other know of plans being used, potential difficulties or achievements so that there would be a continuity between school and home. Without the communication

network James would get mixed signals about expectations, consequences and therapies. I would
also volunteer on a regular basis in the school
library and as a playground and lunchroom
monitor. This gave me the chance to see James and
the other children in action. I knew who the
bullies were and who was a kind child. When
social issues arose I knew who was who and had a
better idea of James' role in any interaction.

It was all a lot of work and often emotionally
exhausting, but James worked hard and made tremendous progress in every way. It was not always
easy, but he was an honors student who was very
committed to his art work. Unfortunately, the
school only went to the fifth grade.

Like many parents, Celia and her husband, John, explored
the option of private schools for their son. The ones in their
area had no resources for special education students and
were not open to accommodating James' learning style.
Public school was the only choice. As in other communities, the town's elementary schools were consolidated into
one large middle school for grades six through eight.
Intense preparations took place for James' transition to this
hectic environment. Details were worked out pertaining to
homeroom placement, the location of his locker, and the
scheduling of classes. The assignment of his five course
teachers was carefully weighed. Students James had a
positive rapport with were placed in his classes. He would
forego physical education and substitute the time with
speech and language therapy from the school's therapist.
His regular, private, therapeutic swim lessons would fulfill
physical education requirements.

At least three times during the summer Celia and James visited the middle school facility. James met with the new speech and language pathologist who was assigned the task of overseeing his school days. A sincere reciprocal attempt was made to develop a bond between James and this teacher in order to give him a sense of security in his new surroundings. A map of the building was obtained and James walked through the halls learning where the library, boys' rooms, office and other important locations were. He had no trouble navigating the large physical layout.

Problem-solving strategies were developed. Secretaries in the office were informed about the importance of processing messages between Celia and the teachers. Everyone concerned felt that an airtight plan was in place to ensure success, but Celia was somehow uncomfortable.

> Before James was to go to the middle school I had a very bad feeling about it. The teachers in both the old school and those involved with his IEP for the new school assured me that all would be fine. They said I had to let him go and I was being over-protective.

Around this time a teacher who had taught at both James' elementary school and the middle school called Celia. She asked if she could come by the house and speak privately. She knew of James' AS and was aware of what a highly intelligent boy he was. She sat down at the kitchen table and stunned Celia by saying:

> Please don't send him to the middle school. It will be bad. Many of the children are cruel and intoler-ant. It's an old building with lots of dark corners

where your son can be tormented. A lot of teachers look the other way. I know because I've taught there. Please don't send him.

Celia appreciated the woman's concern, but felt she was exaggerating. Certainly things wouldn't be that bad. There was no other place where James could go to school. The fact that this new information corroborated Celia's gut feelings was surely just a coincidence. James started grade six with an upbeat approach, a willingness to learn and a sincere wish to make friends.

There is a lot to adjust to at a middle school. A large student population, changing classes, five or more classrooms on different floors, various teaching styles, lockers, homeroom and bustling hallways are just some of the hurdles that all students must overcome. An Asperger's person who requires predictability can have a hard time getting used to the fast-paced atmosphere. There were always surprises for James such as substitute teachers and unannounced schedule changes. It soon became apparent to Celia that the communication efforts that had worked so well in past years were now going to be nearly impossible to implement. The sixth grade networking plans looked good in the written IEP, but the logistics of dealing with so many teachers in such a large school were impractical. Teachers at the elementary level had correctly treated Celia and John as an integral part of James' educational team. As she began her early attempts to coordinate home with the new school, Celia felt that she was viewed as an intrusive parent rather than a wealth of information on AS and James.

The speech and language pathologist diligently tried to coordinate the IEP and enforce the communication plan, but she was just one person. She dealt with teachers who were either overwhelmed by the volume of students or firmly entrenched in the belief that they possessed all the answers when it came to what a student needed. In addition to the frustrations Celia was experiencing, James discovered that he had entered an entirely new atmosphere where young teens had little tolerance for anyone with any type of difference. The kind teacher who had visited Celia was right. The middle school was no place for a boy like James. Celia poignantly remembers:

> James is by nature a gentle person. After school I would pick him up to bring him home. He would start releasing the day's stress as soon as he got into the car and shut the door. The crying, yelling and bad moods would continue for hours. He worked so hard to hold himself together at school that the release of pent-up emotion would be like a volcano erupting. He would be beside himself and it would take me a long time to calm him down.

She describes a situation that many families experience. AS students work so hard to handle their environment during the school day that they sometimes take out their frustrations on things or loved ones as soon as they get home. One mother described her seventh grade daughter as actually becoming physically abusive in a frantic attempt to get rid of the day's stresses.

Celia found that by listening carefully to her son she developed a fairly good idea of how his days were going at school. He was not able to follow what was going on in classes because he was so distracted. The large number of students, noise level and variety of teaching styles through-out the day made it hard for James to focus on information that was being presented. When his confusion became obvious, he was ridiculed by fellow students. Celia discovered that some of these students were using school as an opportunity to vent frustrations over issues they were unable to manage in their own lives.

Although he possessed a very high IQ, James needed extra explaining when it came to math. As a result, he had been placed at the lowest math level. Explanation here was very thorough, but the class was a catch-all for students with behavior problems. James was so bombarded with the poor behavior of his math classmates that he did not have the capacity to absorb any information. The response of the special education department was that this was the best math setting for James within the school and the only one in which his needs could be addressed.

Asperger's children have trouble letting go of a slight, whether real or perceived. Any unkind deed or comment is locked in their memory forever. James was being picked on at school, not only in math class, but throughout the day. Some children did approach him with the intention of being friendly, but he was so distraught from negative interactions that he couldn't see kindness when it was offered. Many of his tormentors were in his classes. Celia recalls:

> How could my son learn being in a room with the children who picked on him? Even if they were absent he would still have difficulty because he was in the very room where the teasing had taken

place. Just seeing them in class constantly
reminded him of past wrongs and he could not
listen to what was being taught by the teacher. He
was too busy reliving the insults and worrying
about the next one that might come his way.

Around this time Celia began confiding her concerns to a
relative who was a teacher. Mary lived in a neighboring
state and had taught varying grades in the same elementary
school for over twenty-five years. Part of that time had been
spent as principal. A very intelligent woman and a committed educator, Mary knew and loved James. She had
followed his progress through elementary school and the
Asperger's diagnosis with unwavering interest. She listened
to Celia and John, spoke with James and confirmed what
they already knew. They were paying a heavy emotional
price for what James was getting out of his middle school
education. She began an effort of keeping in touch with
Celia weekly.

Each day Celia had to reteach at home what had been
presented in class. This could only take place when James
had been calmed down after a long day at school. The
afternoon would be completely spent between the calming
efforts and reteaching. After dinner James would need to
begin his homework. Bringing out the homework
reminded him of the day's difficulties and any tranquility
that had been achieved was quickly gone.

Celia was able to discern a great deal about her son's
school days by simply waiting in the parking lot to pick
him up. She relates:

> I saw a boy I knew to be a bully open a school door
> from the inside and push another boy down the

> outside stairs. The bully shut the door so the victim was stuck outside. I knew this bully targeted my son. I could only imagine what he was doing to James.

Another day as she was waiting, Celia observed a physical education class finish up outside. As the students headed back toward the school building, two boys started teasing a smaller boy from the class. It was unpleasant to witness but what was even more disturbing was that Celia could see the phys ed instructor watching the entire scenario. He did nothing to stop it. This was precisely what had been predicted by the concerned teacher who visited her.

Two trouble spots that emerged were lunchtime and art class. Lunch was understandable because the cafeteria was so noisy and confusing. Arrangements were made for James to eat in the quieter guidance office. This did not work out as students being disciplined for poor behavior in the cafeteria would be sent to this office for punishment. James had no place where he could go to eat in peace. Art class was a difficulty no one expected. The art teacher was very encouraging, but other students saw how seriously James took his work and how he reacted to anyone making fun of art. They saw this as a weakness and used the subject to provoke him. Teachers tried to capitalize on his talents by asking him to paint a mural in a hallway. James couldn't negotiate working on a ladder and had never painted anything that large before. He was unable to complete the project. He viewed the unfinished mural as an example of an art failure. Celia and John always hoped that James would find a career in the field of art. They were afraid that under the present circumstances their son's enthusiasm for the subject would be lost and they would lose their chance to develop his one main talent.

James was quickly losing his sense of value. He seemed to be in a constant state of overload. This intelligent boy who showed so much promise with his art was shell-shocked. He found it impossible to implement any of the social strategies he had been taught in such an unwieldy atmosphere. Teachers assured his parents that James was doing fine and that the IEP was being implemented. Celia kept thinking, however, about how much James was putting into just making it through each school day. Although his grades were good, she felt that he wasn't learning all that much compared to the effort that went into managing the environment. His IQ was so high and his quality of life within school was so low that she was extremely uncomfortable with the entire situation.

> I felt like I was betraying him. Every day before he left home I assured him that the day would be great. I would tell him that he could handle whatever came up if he just employed the strategies we had worked out. We had extensively used scripting with the speech and language pathologist to give him words to use when trouble came up. I would remind him of what to say, even writing cue words on his hands. I remember sitting in the car after dropping him off at school and watching him go up the stairs and through the door into the building. I felt my heart sinking because I knew his day would be awful. I felt he deserved better. He deserved a little happiness. There wasn't much happiness.

Celia has tremendous respect for the incredible courage James displayed at this time. She doesn't know how he reached down inside himself and got the inner strength to walk up those school steps every day.

> There were teachers who really did care, but they couldn't make up for those who didn't and for the overpowering negativity of each school day. I had this feeling deep down inside that all the work that had gone into James over the past years was being undone.

Years ago James' kindergarten teacher had told Celia, "Listen to your gut. If you follow your inner voice, you're never wrong." Those words kept haunting Celia as the inner voice that was warning her before James started the middle school continued to gnaw at her. She relates:

> There was no doubt we were suffering. I was so stressed that I had no life. I would go through so much emotion and anxiety boosting my son's spirits to get him off to school that I would be emotionally drained from just getting him there.

The day Celia believed she got the true picture was when she brought Temple Grandin's book *Thinking In Pictures* to the school's guidance counselor. This person was assigned the task of helping James negotiate some of the daily social minefields. She planned to donate the book to the guidance department in an effort to help the counselor understand her son more. As soon as she handed it to him, she knew that she had wasted her money. He made a sarcastic comment about the book without even knowing what it was about. "I immediately knew that this man was not, and never would be, on our wavelength," she remembers.

Encountering the guidance counselor's attitude was a defining moment. Celia suddenly realized that for months her own inner guidance system had been screaming at her and she had failed to acknowledge it. Thoughts that had been incoherent suddenly began to gel in her mind. "I became acutely aware of just how sick I was of the daily struggle," she recalls. "If I was sick of it, I could only imagine how James felt." She also came to see that John had been silently enduring hardships brought on by the pervasive influence of the middle school.

John had his own business and Celia would often work at his office assisting the secretary, running errands or filling in when employees were out. She was no longer able to do this which caused a backlog in several important projects. John found that when James had a bad day at school there was a ripple effect throughout the house. If Celia had to spend time calming down their son and reteaching material, then other general daily tasks would not have been accomplished and nerves would be worn. Homework assignments caused further agony and less time for positive family interaction and communication. The situation was unpleasant and difficult.

Looking back at their own school experiences, the couple remembered how hard it was for each of them to fit in during the teen years. Addressing their own memories caused them to have greater compassion for what James was going through. They also noticed that most of the knowledge he acquired came from his own general reading, interests, interaction with family contacts and news. None of it really came from school. It was apparent that James and his parents were putting more into school than he was getting out of it. Celia says:

> I felt that our existence was a tortured one. A great fear we had was that because of cruel peers James would have no self-esteem left. We were afraid that all the love, resources and hard work that had been directed toward him would be undone. The adolescents he was exposed to seemed to function in predatory packs as a result of the peer pressure to fit in and be accepted. I didn't want my son to continue being one of their victims.
>
> Members of the school team kept assuring me that their way was the road to success. Everyone who said they knew what was best for my son would go on with their careers and then retire. They moved on with their lives whether or not they failed with James, but what would his life be like? John and I would have to pick up the pieces. Unhappiness had permeated our family life and daily outlook. This wasn't living. This was a test of how much my son and I could endure on a daily basis.

Celia knew no one who homeschooled, but had become somewhat aware of it through a few newspaper and magazine articles. She did know that it was legal in all fifty states. She had never considered it before, but now necessity was forcing her to be open to anything that might provide relief to the current situation. During one of her weekly phone conversations with Mary, Celia told her relative that she was considering home education for James.

The veteran teacher and principal enthusiastically responded, "Why not?"

Celia called the Department of Education in her state capital. There was a person there who worked exclusively with homeschooling families. The necessary forms for withdrawing James from school were sent to Celia and she filled them out. She learned of a statewide homeschooling coalition and called contact members. Through suggested reading and parent contacts she developed confidence for what she was about to do.

Note

1. PDD-NOS (Pervasive Developmental Disorder – Not Otherwise Specified).

CHAPTER TWO

The Road Home

It was almost the end of sixth grade. Celia and John made the decision to remove James from the middle school and educate him at home. They looked into homeschool curriculums and learned about some excellent ones from home education guide books available in their local library and bookstores. One was chosen from an accredited, established correspondence school. Celia made an appointment with the superintendent of schools, went to his office armed with information about what James would be studying and completed paperwork for withdrawing him from the school system.

The superintendent was a gentle, open-minded man who respected the decision to homeschool James. He recognized that John and Celia were conscientious people who would educate their son well and he was very enthusiastic about the quality of the chosen curriculum. He did express concern, however, that homeschooling would limit James' opportunities for socialization. This struck a nerve of concern and got Celia's mind whirling about the choices she was making. The confidence she brought with her into the meeting started to melt away. Once again that inner voice was screaming, but she tuned it out. The superintendent made an important point about socialization.

For all his successes, James' social limitations were obvious. Celia became terribly confused between what she knew in her heart to be the right thing and what she was being told by an educational expert. She agreed with many of the theories about homeschooling that she had been reading about, but her son had AS. He needed social contact in order to learn how to function in the world. The fact that the socialization at school was seriously damaging James made this dilemma almost unbearable to Celia.

The superintendent said that some other districts in the state were trying shared schooling. He thought this might address the socialization issue. He asked what Celia's weakest subjects were and she informed him that math and science were troublesome. He suggested that James take those two courses at the middle school and continue to receive speech and language services. Celia would homeschool all other subjects through the chosen curriculum. James would spend substantially less time in the school each day which would eliminate his high stress level, yet he would still have the opportunity to interact with people his own age. It sounded reasonable.

After talking it over with John and James, it was agreed that James would begin seventh grade taking math and science at the middle school. Celia would homeschool all other subjects using the purchased curriculum she had chosen. Speech and language services would continue. James was open and positive about this new approach to his education. He began seventh grade looking forward to the reduced time at school.

A schedule was developed around the timing of James' math and science classes. Times were also set aside each week for speech and language therapy. James and Celia worked on homeschool material in the morning. Math class was held at 10:00 a.m. so they worked until it was time for James to be driven to school. Class would last for about forty-five minutes. There was not enough time to drive home and come back to school again, so Celia would either wait in the car or spend the time at a nearby coffee shop. When math was over, James would come out to the car to pass forty-five minutes until it was time for science. They started off the year trying to wisely use the time between the two courses. James would have a snack and Celia would read out loud to him from whatever novel they were studying for homeschool. She felt tethered to her car for extensive periods of time and her mobility was very restricted by James' coming and going.

Juggling times was complicated, but they managed. What soon emerged were the same old issues that plagued them when James was in the sixth grade. Although there were just two teachers this year, Celia was still explaining AS and making efforts to communicate with the school. James continued to be harassed by other students. Simply being within the middle school building brought back a flood of memories to him of the previous year's unhappiness. This new school year, despite the home education component, was no improvement.

The science teacher was pleased to have James as a pupil and willing to work hard to help him have a successful year. There was a student within the class, however, who had very serious emotional problems. He ridiculed James and would cause scenes in front of the entire class, calling him inhuman and referring to him as "the thing." The science teacher had his hands full controlling this student plus trying to teach a lesson. He had no time to focus in on how James felt after these humiliations. James was not learning much in science class. The math teacher was the same one as the prior year. Once again, this was the lowest math level with the additional explanations James needed and there were no other choices. Just as before, this class had many students who had behavioral problems.

Once again James was coming out of school distraught and Celia would have to calm him down. She had hoped that the pent-up stress would not be as severe this year because of the reduced amount of time within the facility. James said that the shared schooling brought more problems for him, not less. Because he was in and out of the school building, the other students were curious about his unusual schedule. When he attempted to explain what he was doing, they made fun of him. The scheduling drew too much attention to him. No reading could take place in the car between classes. The entire time had to be used to coax James back into the building for science. They would go home after science, but no homeschool work could be started until he had adequate time to decompress.

Celia felt that her family was still drowning in the same unhappiness of the year before. She and James loved their home courses and worked well together, but running back and forth to the middle school made progress excruciatingly slow. Celia was still calming James, communicating with teachers, running interference, and reteaching math and science courses. She continued to remain in weekly contact with Mary. Although initially intrigued with the concept of shared schooling, the experienced teacher now agreed with Celia's determination that it was not working for James.

The theory was that the limited amount of time spent at the middle school would help James manage the social stresses of his environment better. The hope was that the overload would be diminished and he could implement what he had learned about the rules of social engagement. The concept was excellent, but the reality was very different. Celia felt that her highly intelligent, artistic son was still trapped in an atmosphere of intolerance and learning little. She knew that she had made a mistake with the shared schooling. She had listened to the superintendent and followed his suggestions. She let her fears about lack of socialization for her Asperger's child cloud her thinking. The superintendent's intentions were good, but he didn't know James or AS the way Celia did.

It didn't matter any more what anyone thought, what the theories were, or how much social interaction James was or was not getting. Celia, John and James were unhappy and James' contact with the school was the source. It had to be eliminated from their lives.

Education should not be about suffering. It should be about learning. It is extremely difficult for an Asperger's student to implement the social strategies he has been taught through therapies if he is in a constant state of bombardment. Many parents of AS children relate that unwanted behaviors develop in their children as a result of the stress the child is placed in daily. As the negative behaviors increase, more therapies are sought to assist in controlling them. Bad things continue to happen at school and the search for more therapies goes on. It is like a dog chasing its tail. Life gets very complicated. One mother of a sixth grader relates how her AS son would be so overwhelmed by school that he would go into a corner of the classroom and get into a fetal position. His aggression toward family members was of great concern. Once she removed her son from school and began home educating him things changed. A lot of the unwanted behaviors seemed to fall away as life became less riddled with fear. AS does not go away, but behaviors brought about by a child living a life of constant trauma can diminish along with the source of the tension.

About three-quarters of the way through the seventh grade, Celia once again went to see the superintendent of schools. Just as before, she went with the paperwork prepared for removing her son from the school system. She had further information on hand about math and science courses available from the correspondence school. The superintendent listened to Celia's description of how shared schooling was going. He understood her desire for a happier life for her family and acknowledged the negative social tone of the middle school. Celia totally withdrew

James from school. The meeting was extremely cordial and the superintendent could not have been more supportive. She still had to go to the middle school and complete paperwork signing off from the services of the speech and language pathologist. Celia immediately drove to the school and located her. The forms were filled out and Celia signed on the signature line.

Unlike her meeting with the superintendent, the tension at school was palpable. Although certainly polite, the pathologist let it be known that she had given her best to James and if things had not worked out, it wasn't her fault. News travels fast and the science teacher quickly popped his head into the room to let Celia know that what she was about to do was, in his opinion, a tragedy. He stated that withdrawing James would ruin him and he would never develop into a well-adjusted person without the social interaction of school. Celia thanked the teacher for his input. She thanked the speech and language pathologist for all she had done for James and left.

For the last time, Celia parked in the school lot and waited for James. He came out of the building and got into the car. As usual, he was very stressed. Celia has vivid recollections of that moment:

> He had just gotten in the car when a student opened a window in an upstairs classroom and yelled out James' name. It was obviously an effort to taunt James. It simply affirmed in my mind that the right decision had been made. I told James that I had withdrawn him from school completely and he didn't have to go back. A look of wonderment came over his face and his joy just filled the car. As

we pulled away from the parking lot I felt, what I can only describe as, a natural high. It was an exhilaration. James said that he felt it also. It was like nothing I had ever felt before. I think it was a feeling of empowerment. It was absolutely incredible. I will remember that feeling for the rest of my life.

CHAPTER THREE

Moving Forward

In the weeks and months following that memorable last trip from the school parking lot, Celia and James developed confidence in homeschooling. The trauma of withdrawing from the system became more and more distant. Now that the pressures of the school day were removed James, Celia and John felt that, for the first time, they were really experiencing life as it was meant to be. There certainly were ups and downs. The challenges of home educating a young person with AS can never be minimized, but the family felt as if it could finally breathe. Celia recalls that during this period she reflected a great deal on the decision that had been made. There was no regret. There was simply a need to process the entire experience. Acknowledging the magnitude of the decision seemed to be part of moving forward into the new kind of lifestyle offered by home education.

John had his own story to tell. The logistics of life required that he be at his business daily and Celia would handle issues involving their AS son, the schools, doctors, therapists etc. John, however, was the great support Celia needed. He was the one to listen to ideas and calm Celia down after she had calmed down James. Committed to his son's education, John was always available for conferences, special meetings with teachers, and science fair projects. It was very hard for him to watch his family being controlled by the school environment. Since the homeschooling began, John felt that Celia was still depending on him, but in a much more pleasant and positive way. He found her asking him to actively participate in James' home education rather than seeking advice about daily school problems. This filled John with enthusiasm. He was no longer simply a mediator and cheerleader for Celia's dealings with the middle school.

Celia and John prided themselves on never having "run with the pack." It bent their natures to participate in a system with such a high emphasis on socialization and mainstreaming. Neither had ever experienced a sense of belonging within their own school communities, but each walked the expected educational paths. They understood the traumas James was exposed to and recognized that his were magnified a thousand times over by AS. So much of their lives had been spent dealing with school stress, first with their own and then their son's. Saying good-bye to such a long-time, looming presence in their world was a life-altering experience.

Celia and John discussed her weak points in creating learning opportunities for James. A definite trouble area was physical education and any sports-related activity. It was decided that James would continue with the therapeutic swim lessons he enjoyed and benefited from and his father would introduce him to new sport experiences. John also became active in organizing family excursions or enrichment activities which were a source of great pleasure. He and James would pore over maps together as they plotted out the best routes to a point of interest in their state. John's role shifted from helping to cope with negatives to creating and enacting positives. As far as the education of his son was concerned, he now had a tremendous amount to happily contribute rather than being on the fringes of an unhappy situation.

Celia knew that a lot of responsibilities came with homeschooling. Although it was somewhat scary, it was also exciting. She was concerned about how she would find resources for an AS student, locate social opportunities and create a homeschool network. She also knew that all the energies she and her family had put into the school setting could now be directed toward addressing these needs. Things could only be better. Shared schooling hadn't worked out, but it gave the family a chance to get its feet wet with home education.They had a good sense of what they were getting into. It allowed them to see that they could work together and get things accomplished. Looking back on all that had happened, Celia knew that she had saved her son's life. She equated withdrawing him from middle school to the Marines going in on a rescue mission to a foreign city somewhere in the world. For the first time in her life she had bucked a system. She didn't do what was expected of her. James was worth putting herself on the line for.

Celia found that the experiences she and James had with the middle school were so unpleasant that it was hard for her to recall the support and positives of the elementary school. Obviously there are intelligent and devoted teachers and kind fellow students. An Asperger's student, however, can perseverate on the negatives. These negatives get so magnified that they loom large over everything. They can block out whatever sunshine may come from upbeat people. James would make positive comments about his teachers from the elementary days, but he would never mention any teachers from the middle school. Unfortunately his latter experience had been so bitter that he lumped the good people in with the not-so-good.

Although it may work well for some families, the shared schooling was a mistake for James and his parents. Celia and John felt that in trying to give the middle school experience a chance, they had stuck it out too long. Celia knew deep down that things were not going to go well right from the beginning. She received a very solid warning from a teacher who had once worked there. Unfortunately she squelched the signals she was getting from her natural radar and listened to functionaries within the school system. Although well-intentioned, none of these individuals knew James the way his parents did, nor did they live daily with AS.

Not a day went by without James saying, "Thank you, Mom, for homeschooling me." Although angry and sad about his time at school, he was glad to have had the experience of what it was like there. He astutely said that if he didn't know what it was like, he wouldn't appreciate how good it was to learn at home. Celia similarly felt that if he hadn't participated in school life, James would have believed that she had deprived him of joining in what everyone else was doing. She refers to the entire middle school episode when saying:

> We tell our children to walk away from bad situations, but then we let them wallow in an environment where they expend too much valuable time and energy just learning to tolerate the intolerable. I feel that by making the decision to homeschool my AS son, I have taught him an important life lesson. If you are in a bad situation, do something about it. You don't have to tolerate mediocrity and unkindness.

Many books about home education state that when the transition is made from school to homeschool, students quite often need some down time to get used to the change. Celia thought that would be the case as James started homeschooling full time. Surprisingly he wanted to jump right in with both feet and get underway immediately. Transitions had always been hard for James because of the AS. This time was different because the change was welcomed. He was no longer being dictated to by a large educational machine. He was now a vital influence in creating his own education.

Celia chose to stay with the same purchased curriculum she used during the days of shared schooling. This was a very structured, accredited correspondence program with a teaching support service that could be called if she was confused about any of the materials or needed back-up on how to present information. Additional courses were added now that math and science were not being taught through the public school. Math was Celia's weak spot. John was very good at it, but he was busy running his business. A tutor was needed to teach the math course. Celia remembered a young man who was student teaching at the middle school. She contacted him and a whole new world of math opened up for James.

Mark was a mathematics major at a nearby state university and had just completed his student teaching. A brilliant student, he planned to stay at the university and go on for his master's degree and Ph.D. He was paying for his own education and needed funds. When Celia approached him about the possibility of teaching James, Mark jumped at the opportunity. The price of tutoring was expensive, but Celia could not teach math. She also felt that Mark would be a positive contact in James' life. It was worth the price. Mark would be James' math tutor for the next five years. James went to the university three times a week for math lessons. He and Mark would meet at various locations, usually the student union or library. When the university closed for holidays, Mark would come to the house. He read about Asperger's, listened to Celia's explanation of it and got to know James.

Since Mark had completed his student teaching at the same school James had attended, he could offer some excellent insights. Like the teacher who had warned Celia about the middle school long ago, Mark was able to offer information with the knowledge of an insider. He believed that the school could be a good environment for many students, but for a boy with AS it would be a nightmare.

Celia didn't need validation for having removed her son from school, but if she had been looking for it, Mark was the person to talk to.

Lessons with Mark were a far cry from the low math group at school with all the behavior problems. James now had one-on-one math instruction. He zoomed through his lessons. It was hard work, but the setting was pleasant and he was willing to put in the effort. Since early childhood he had enjoyed drawing extremely complex geometric shapes and patterns. Mark was able to touch upon this interest and through him James was able to meet two well known mathematicians visiting the university. Both men were recognized for their work with patterns that were of interest to James. He was thrilled to have met them. When James completed his high school studies, he was functioning solidly at the college math level.

James took a full load of courses through the correspondence school. In addition, he took two art classes at a local creative arts studio. These were given in the late afternoon or early evening. One was a teen art class and the other involved mostly adults. Sandra taught both courses. She immediately sensed James' artistic talents and was very willing to learn about AS. Sandra worked hard to get James beyond his dislike of messes. She got him to try difficult mediums such as oils and watercolors. He developed a great fondness for her and, because of the comfort level he experienced in her classes, was able to broaden his art horizons tremendously. The classes gave him an opportunity to meet some young people around his own age as well as older people who were doing more advanced work. No one made fun of James for being artistic. As with the math lessons, James remained a student at this studio for about five years.

The math and art lessons took up quite a bit of time. Celia and James found that they had to make a concerted effort to stay at home for quiet times to complete lessons for the various courses. A daily schedule was developed which revolved around math, art and the ongoing therapeutic swim lessons. James helped his mother make up the schedule. Working on it enabled him to learn about managing time and assuming responsibility for his day. The schedule was important and James felt in control by having some input. Celia didn't care in what order work was done, as long as it was given enough time. This included time to present material, discuss it and do assignments.

Over the years James benefited from a great deal of intense intervention from both private and school therapists who concentrated on sensory and language issues. Now that he was home-educated, the services obtained through the school system were no longer available. The situation had changed, however, as James grew older and many of his sensory integration issues dissipated. Whatever techniques were needed to help James had already been learned by the family. What was currently required along these lines could be done at home.

There could never be enough speech and language therapy, however, and James would always need assistance navigating the nuances of the social world. From another mother in the area Celia learned of a speech and language pathologist who would come to the house on an as-needed basis. The woman was familiar with AS and had other Asperger's clients. She would visit twice a month. She worked out programs for James depending on the issues he was struggling with. He would work on these himself until her next visit.

Parents who homeschool Asperger's children often comment that many negative behaviors fall away when their children are removed from the schools. James' social limitations continued to exist, but because his new circumstances were less tumultuous, he was able to function better socially. He received a greater volume of therapy in school, but needed more because of his surroundings. The new homeschool environment was one of reduced stress where he could practice and implement the instructions of the speech and language pathologist.

The costs of the correspondence school were not particularly expensive, but the math instruction, art lessons, therapeutic swim, and speech and language services certainly were. In spite of all the responsibility of a mother involved in home education, Celia occasionally was able to put in a little work time at John's office and that was a bit of a help. Expenses were definitely very tight. The good news was that James, Celia and John were happy. No price could be put on the wonderful feeling they all had of doing something to help themselves. Celia didn't mind driving her older car with over two hundred thousand miles on it. It got her where she needed to go. The cost of lessons was still a lot cheaper than a private school. The expenses wouldn't go on forever and their new life was worth every single penny.

CHAPTER FOUR

Socialization

This is known in homeschooling circles as "the big S word." People who are not familiar with homeschooling, and those just getting started with it, find socialization to be a tremendous issue. Concern about a lack of social opportunities keeps many families from considering home education. Parents of Asperger's children have serious and legitimate reasons to ponder this subject. The question to be asked is socialization with whom and for what purpose?

Families are told that the AS child must learn to function within the school system because it will teach the child skills for living in the real world. Teachers, doctors, family members and friends tell parents that school is a microcosm of reality and children need the experience of getting along with others. It is believed that removing the AS child from this reality would deprive him of the necessary lessons about how to live in society. Rather than believing that socialization is a reason for sending children to school, most homeschooling families feel that today's socialization is the ultimate reason for *not* placing a child in school. For the AS child, school socialization is not always learning how to get along with others, but rather a test of how much negativity can be endured in one day.

Parents work hard to ensure their AS children get the right kind of therapies in order to learn social functioning. Children get these services either through the schools or privately. Oftentimes it is a combination of both. There are many skilled therapists providing excellent services to help Asperger's children learn how to be part of the world around them. The problem is that many lessons learned from therapists are thrown out the window when the AS student is overwhelmed by the type of social activity usually present in school settings.

AS is, in many ways, a social disability. Oftentimes parents over-emphasize socialization as they are pressured into putting their AS child in the wrong situations. People will say that parents cannot micromanage their child's contacts throughout his life. Certainly no AS parent wants to do that. Most parents want a break from the strain of having an Asperger's child and want to see that child independent and functioning well socially. It is necessary, however, to provide an environment that is set up to nurture happiness and positive social development.

For Celia and other AS parents, finding positive social opportunities is a tremendous burden. The parent is always a buffer between society and what will upset their child. This becomes extremely wearing, especially as it continues year after year. An AS child who is miserable in school has a miserable parent. The parent functions as the go-between for the Asperger's student, teachers, educational hierarchy and the often unwelcoming social setting. In the midst of all this, it is easy to lose sight of who you and your child really are. It is hard, as a homeschooling parent, to locate all the right social opportunities for your student. It is easier, however, than trying to undo daily the strain and damage caused by the social hardships faced in school. When the AS child comes home from spending the day in a stress-filled atmosphere, he takes it out on the family. Everyone suffers.

Critics of home education say that school provides a view of reality that will toughen the youngster up for life in a harsh world. Homeschooling parents question whether or not school actually is a lesson in reality. It may prove to be a lesson in unreality and cause poor behavior as a result. Reality does not consist of socializing exclusively with people of your own age group for six hours a day. This promotes a pack mentality and an increase in peer pressure. Homeschooling can provide social contact in more natural settings with better results.

Home education gives the AS student time to think and process the many therapies being received. One mother who started homeschooling her AS son took advantage of his interest in animals. He volunteered to help out weekly at a local animal shelter. Although he loved animals, he was afraid of horses. After a few weeks of the combination of homeschooling and volunteering, he asked if he could take horseback riding lessons. He now participates in a thera-peutic horseback riding program and benefits greatly from it. He is getting socialization at the shelter with others who work there. He is also getting socialization from the riding program. Both are positive settings with people who have a similar interest in animals. They appreciate him for volunteering and respect his interest. He is meeting other children who have differences. He is needed and not ostracized.

As James got into the routine of homeschooling he was very busy with obligations outside of the home. Celia found that they had to schedule time to complete course work. James had math lessons three times a week and therapeutic swim once a week. At each lesson he was meeting and interacting with people. Celia also discovered that each and every outing to a dentist office, barber shop or store was an opportunity for socialization. There was time now to be less rushed which gave James a chance to do some of his own shopping and transactions in stores and restaurants.

Celia and John noticed that as the hardships of school went away, James came out of his trauma-induced shell. He became more social than he had ever been in his life. They felt this was because he was no longer in forced socialization with people he didn't want to be with. He was less fearful and his eye contact improved. He would always have AS, but he was more comfortable with himself. Through one of his art classes James even met a young lady his own age named Abby. Abby became James' girlfriend for a while. An unusual person, she and James seemed to sense each other's differences. After talking with Celia and being directed to the right doctors, this friend received a diagnosis of Asperger's Syndrome.

Many critics complain that the homeschooler will never learn to work in a group setting if the student is home all day. They wonder how the homeschooling parent can provide the experience of working toward a goal with a team of people. James and Abby had a wonderful and memorable experience through their teen art class which provided just such an opportunity. The local arts center where their classes were held decided to participate in the town's annual Christmas parade. A float had to be designed and built. The teen art class volunteered for the job. The theme was Christmas past and present. John built a portion of the float on a friend's flatbed truck. The art students created the rest out of a wide variety of materials and lots of cooperation. Students from the dancing school associated with the center danced behind the float as it traveled down Main Street with Christmas music from the 1950s blasting. Dancing on the float itself were James and Abby dressed in 1950s attire, waving to the hundreds and hundreds of people who turned out for the big parade.

James and Abby were vital parts of a team led by Sandra, their capable art teacher. Two Asperger's teens took this project from its inception to actually taking the float apart after the parade. It was an opportunity to successfully participate in a group effort. There were obstacles and tense moments, but thanks to the determination of Sandra and her class, the undertaking was a tremendous achievement.

Asperger's children who are homeschooled don't just stay home. They are active people learning socialization skills in everyday settings. Because they are not burdened by the unkindness and ostracism of the schools, the lessons learned in therapies can be recalled and implemented in a more comfortable way. James' participation in the teen art class allowed him to be with young people his own age. The adult art group allowed him to be with more advanced artists. Both groups offered him the chance to be with different types of people, some pleasant and some not so pleasant.

An unpleasant person in a small music, drama or art class that meets at a local center may provide a greater chance to practice learned social strategies than a multitude of unpleasant adolescents day after day for hours at a time. Since time moves at a less pressured rate when homeschooling, James had plenty of opportunities to discuss with his parents any confusions that arose. He seemed to digest the lessons he received from his speech and language pathologist and remember them better than he had when he was continually exposed to the social dynamics of middle school.

One mother of an AS teen relates how her socially awkward daughter had stones thrown at her and was continually tripped at school. Any self-esteem the girl possessed was quickly eroding. She could not implement learned strategies because she was always anxiously anticipating the next bit of cruelty. As soon as she was removed from school and started taking control of her own education, she relaxed and was able to practice social skills. She is happier now and has become a great self-advocate.

An Asperger's student who is a sophomore was recently beaten up in a boys' room at his high school. His glasses were broken and he was injured as a result of being slammed against tile walls. His life is so unbearable from bullying that he says he has no worth and wants to commit suicide. He learns little because of his fear and depression. His parents continue to send him to school because he needs socialization. What price will their son ultimately pay in order to be socialized in today's schools?

Self-esteem that is destroyed in youth is hard to reclaim in adulthood. This is true for all students, but even more so for those with AS who muster tremendous courage each and every day just to walk through the school door. In a pubescent environment where those with any differences are frowned upon, the sensitive AS teen is shunned. The encouragement of self-esteem provides the foundation for implementing Asperger's therapies. The opportunities to boost self-worth in school may be present from time to time, but they are fleeting.

Prior to withdrawing James from school, Celia had tremendous concerns about how he perceived himself. He was in school for six hours a day with overly judgmental middle schoolers. James knew no one who had interests similar to his. He felt very alone. What became the symbol of this predicament was James' shirts. He hated to have his shirt untucked, but at school all the boys had their shirts hanging out of their pants. James was teased for having his shirt tucked in. Celia found herself telling him to leave his shirt out so he would visually blend in with the crowd and be less of a target. It dawned on her that if he compromised on a little thing like tucking in his shirt to get along, then what lesson was he learning about the bigger issues in life? Would he learn that he would have to give in on the issues of sex, alcohol, drugs and poor behaviors in order to blend in? Would he suppress his talents and interests because they were unusual? Celia decided that being true to himself was the most important lesson James could learn.

Life is full of bullies of one sort or another. They will never be in short supply. The homeschooled student just doesn't encounter the volume of them. There are troublesome people in extended families and neighborhoods. The difference is that in a middle school setting the AS student is continually confronted by them. A homeschooled AS student experiences social negatives in smaller doses. He can take each unpleasant experience and use it as a learning platform.

James had just such an opportunity involving a neighborhood family with a teenage son who claimed to be a Nazi. This was a tremendous concern to James who prides himself on his sense of tolerance and social justice. Although he had no interaction with this individual, just knowing that someone of such a mind-set was present in the neighborhood bothered James. Working through this social stress provided him with an intense and difficult learning experience.

Celia, John and James had always spent the holidays with certain relatives. There was never a great bond with these people, yet because they were family an effort was made to share some special times. These individuals had never tried to understand AS and were quite critical of James. Celia tried to overlook some of their comments in an effort to keep family peace. After homeschooling for a number of months and feeling more and more confident about himself, James informed his parents that he saw no sense in spending precious holiday time with people they did not particularly enjoy. He thought it made more sense to design some new holiday traditions involving other people in their lives who were more understanding. John and Celia looked at each other, recognizing that James was right. They were amazed that they hadn't come to this conclusion themselves. Changes were made and holidays are much more pleasurable. Celia and John believe that their son took a lesson from the experience of deciding to homeschool. He saw himself in an uncomfortable situation. He recognized that he did not have to put up with it and could do something about it. Thanks to his ideas, holiday time is much happier and he was able to take the lead on initiating positive change.

The goal in home educating an AS youngster is to feed him varied social settings in manageable doses. Many of these settings will be in areas of interest to the Asperger's student, such as the boy who volunteered at an animal shelter and took horseback riding lessons. Within these varied settings will be positive and negative people, just as there are in school. These doses of exposure to the negative are on a reduced level giving the AS person the chance to actually handle them. At the same time, the positive is accentuated by being in smaller groups centered around mutual interest. Life presents plenty of unpleasant lessons from which to learn. These range from the cantankerous relative no one wants to see coming up the walk to intolerant neighbors to that arrogant teen at the local arts center. Even a rude cashier at the grocery store provides a lesson in how to handle a negative.

Young homeschoolers with AS can benefit from exposure to all of these situations. When the Asperger's student is not under continual fire from an unsuitable social situation, he can learn to manage the difficulties presented in everyday living. Homeschooling provides opportunities for functional socialization and that is the critical difference from socialization in school. An abundance of quiet times present in home education will never do the damage of reduced self-esteem caused by unkind peers.

CHAPTER FIVE

Making It All Work

It is one thing to be full of terrific ideas about homeschooling a young person with AS and another thing to actually make it all work.

Parents talk of the unforgettable experience of looking at their child on that first day at home and wondering what they had gotten themselves into. The important thing to remember is that all homeschooling parents feel this way from time to time. The key to success is having a plan and recognizing that it may have to be changed according to what does or does not work. There is no such thing as a learning disability in home education and no need to accentuate differences. You and your child simply do what needs to be done for learning to take place.

Parents embarking on this road must establish for themselves an information network. The network should consist of doctors and therapists expert in AS as well as local and statewide homeschool organizations that can provide direction, support and advice in the arena of home learning. Take what is helpful from these sources and what suits your purposes. No one person or group has all the answers for you, but by networking and listening you can obtain the information you need.

Although homeschooling is legal in all fifty states, different states have different regulations. Your local homeschool organization or its website can provide a copy of your state law regarding home education and suggestions about how to comply with it. Also, the Department of Education in your state capital can provide information to prospective homeschooling families. It is a good idea to check a number of sources to make sure that you get a clear picture of what is required.

When you contact a statewide homeschooling group, ask if there is a particular person within the organization who is knowledgeable about your state law and the issue of compliance. There may even be someone who helped write the law. Usually such groups monitor activity within state government that may broaden or infringe upon the rights of homeschooling families. It is important to make your contacts so that you are informed and confident. You not only need to set your child up for success, but yourself as well. By establishing your network you are creating your own platform from which to operate securely, intelligently and happily.

Check your homeschooling groups to locate other parents who are home educating children of varying needs. Certainly not everyone will be aware of AS, but it can be helpful to at least know there are other parents out there who may have chosen home for reasons similar to your own. It is also of interest to know what services, if any, other children are receiving as well as how families of special needs children may be handling the year end evaluations required of all homeschoolers.

When Celia first started educating James, she joined a small support group in her town. She didn't feel comfortable in this group. Everyone was very nice, but they were all younger mothers who were homeschooling their children from the outset. Through this group, however, she learned of a much larger and more influential statewide home education coalition which helped to write the homeschooling law in her state and monitored the educational rights of families very closely. She joined the coalition and through their publications and conferences learned about her rights as a home educator. She made some excellent contacts, particularly one very helpful gentleman who provided tremendous encouragement and guidance about what help to expect and not expect from districts, how to submit a planned curriculum, manage evaluations, and correspond with superintendents. Once Celia got the needed information about her state, she felt confident and empowered.

All homeschooling families must submit a yearly prospective curriculum to what is called a participating agent. The contact for this purpose is a designated person within the district. The submission may vary from a simple listing of subjects to be covered and texts to be used to a detailed agenda, depending on the requirements where you live. When the plan is submitted, it is a good idea to put in writing that you are reserving the right to make changes to it during the course of the year. This gives you freedom to make alterations based upon the needs of your Asperger's student. If a particular text, subject, or program is not working, you have to be free to go with what will be effective. State homeschooling groups can be extremely helpful in providing advice and direction in this regard.

Homeschool fairs offer an opportunity to purchase used books and other materials cheaply. Home education does not have to be an expensive proposition and many parents enjoy the challenge of seeing how inexpensively they can educate their children. The utilization of used or borrowed materials does not indicate inferior learning. Many schools use antiquated texts. It used to upset James that the geography book he was using in school was older than he was. The lack of accuracy about new countries irritated him and made him not want to do the required reading. The book had been marked and abused which reminded him of the lack of respect at school. Celia was able to provide newer geography texts that were a pleasure to him.

Some parents focus a curriculum around the special interest of their Asperger's child. An example of this is an AS boy who was recently withdrawn from his middle school. He has a preoccupation with birds. His mother created a program for him emphasizing the environment and bird habitats for science, birds from various parts of the world for geography, and writing projects centered around his favorite topic. Obviously other subjects are presented, but the special interest acts as a motivator. When his preoccupation ends and he moves onto a new interest, he will be approaching it with a greater knowledge of the environment, geography, wildlife and writing. There are concerns about placing too much emphasis on the current preoccupation of the AS student. However, this strategy can help with the transition to home learning. A gradual weaning away from the subject can take place after routines and expectations have been established at home.

Other families use purchased curriculums from correspondence schools. This is the route that Celia chose for a variety of reasons. She had found the decision to homeschool a monumental one and put so much of herself into just making the decision that she didn't have the energy to create her own curriculum. Another reason, and one many parents of AS homeschoolers cite, is that she and James needed the imposed structure of a more formal program.

A tremendous amount of information exists about home education products available for purchase. Any good bookstore or library has books that provide thorough listings of curriculums, individual courses, materials, and complete correspondence packages. Your local and state-wide homeschooling support groups are also a good information source. Quite often the larger state groups publish directories. They can provide tips on curriculum choices, how to withdraw your child from school, write letters to superintendents, link up with smaller local groups and handle yearly evaluations. Even if you don't want to actively participate in a statewide organization, it is good to join. Newsletters are usually published that keep members informed about tutors, group excursions, lessons offered and upcoming activities in your area. Annual curriculum fairs are a great way to view texts, talk to representatives of various correspondence schools and meet other families

interested in home education. You find out about such
events through newsletters.

As they began homeschooling full time, Celia chose to
stick with the curriculum she had been using when James
was doing the shared schooling. It was an excellent one
that was extremely structured. James needed structure or
things just didn't get done. She liked the fact that the correspondence school kept a transcript of James' grades which
was formal proof of his ongoing educational progress.
Another feature was that the plan was fully accredited.
Many homeschool programs are not. Self-created
programs are, of course, not accredited either.

Celia remembers:

> I felt that, in many ways, the Asperger's put him at
> a disadvantage in the world. I knew that it would
> be important for him to have a diploma from an
> accredited program. I didn't want him to have a
> diploma that would not be recognized by any
> colleges later on. I thought it would just be one
> more thing working against him. In my heart I
> would have loved to create our own plan and go
> with it, but I felt it was an advantage for my
> Asperger's son to be with a recognized correspon-
> dence school.

Many families do not share this opinion and believe it is an
advantage not to have the requirements of a correspondence school imposed upon their child. This is a personal
choice. Today many colleges recognize the value of admit-
ting homeschooled students and it is not necessary to use
accredited programs. Celia went with the security of the

correspondence school believing that the teaching support service it offered provided her with additional backup.

She also felt that the structure of the courses would take the onus off her as far as imposing educational discipline was concerned. The monthly schedule for lesson submissions would provide a framework to keep James moving forward with his studies. Celia wanted her son to be less pressured, but she realized that he needed to know that there were expectations and goals to be met. Knowing that the correspondence school was waiting for the next lesson to be submitted kept James motivated. Families not participating in a program say that their children are challenged by the pleasure of learning for learning's sake and do not need these prompts.

One mother and daughter developed a combination of the two approaches which proved to be a tremendous success. Elizabeth was diagnosed with AS when she was about fourteen. She was so miserable in a public middle school that her single mother pulled her out and placed her in a small local religious school. This setting was fine for a while, but Elizabeth had interests far beyond what was being taught at the school. She was also unhappy socially. Easily offended, quiet and possessing unusual mannerisms, she was often teased. The strict curriculum offered no opportunity for her to pursue her real love. Elizabeth was fascinated by herbs.

Elizabeth's mother created a plan in which she could continue to work and her daughter could study at home, learn to be an herbalist and earn a certified diploma. She heard of a well-known, accredited correspondence program that helps parents develop a curriculum centered around their child's specific interest. Credit is given for special projects and courses taken independently. These credits are combined with ones given for regular course work through the program and a diploma can be issued. The youngster learns important grade level basics and, at the same time, is allowed to pursue real life goals. The pursuit of the interest is a great motivator and Elizabeth moved rapidly through her studies. A few towns away was an herbal farm and educational center run by a certified herbalist. A program of study was developed with the herbalist overseeing Elizabeth's work. The correspondence school was informed about goals and progress. In the meantime, while her mother was at her place of employment, Elizabeth worked on either the herbal studies or regular course work, depending on what had been agreed upon for that particular day.

Elizabeth changed dramatically. After a long day at school she would sometimes physically lash out at her mother or else pace back and forth in her room reliving the day's hurts. Once she adapted to the home education program and was allowed to pursue her true interests, she became a more pleasant person to be around. The Asperger's will always be present, but she is a happier girl working hard to get her diploma and herbal certification.

Just as all homeschoolers must submit a prospective agenda for the upcoming homeschool year, all must be annually evaluated to confirm that educational progress is being made. Usually families can choose between two types of evaluations. One type is standardized testing. The type of test, who administers it, and the location of testing vary and it is best to check with your local district as well as your state and local homeschool support groups to find out more particulars.

The second type of evaluation is the portfolio review and this seems to work beautifully for many homeschooled Asperger's students. AS young people do not always respond well to pressured, timed testing. The portfolio review removes the tension associated with exams. Again, circumstances vary from state to state, but generally the process is the same. A certified teacher of your choice comes into the home and reviews the work done for the year. This is really quite simple. It can be made even better by utilizing a teacher you and your child know well, possibly a neighbor, family friend or teacher from your child's past. Homeschooling newsletters often have advertisements placed by teachers who are willing to do portfolio evaluations. Many of these people are home educating their own children. It is probably wise, however, to choose someone with a knowledge of AS who can understand how you and your child operate.

Celia asked Lorraine, who had been James' third grade teacher. Lorraine had developed a close bond with James and a friendship with his mother. She knew how James learned and was supportive of the decision to go with home education. Throughout James' homeschooling years Lorraine would come to the house once a year and review the work he had done. The papers, texts and miscellaneous materials would be presented in an orderly arrangement on the dining room table. Lorraine would sit down with Celia and look at the work from every subject. She would take notes and later type up a letter to the participating agent indicating whether or not she felt that academic progress was being made. Celia would review the letter before it was submitted to make sure she agreed with the contents.

It is important to check with your homeschool network to learn the exact procedures required in your state before you do the portfolio review. Since the regulations of each area can be different, it is crucial to get good local information. Start early to locate an evaluator and if you find someone you like, then stick with that person. After doing the portfolio review once, the procedure is extremely easy to follow and virtually stress-free for the Asperger's student.

The homeschool support network available to you in your town and state serves another purpose. Most families who home educate do so without difficulties from the local education officials. Sometimes, however, problems do arise and it is important to know your rights. There are many individuals in the world of education who are not open-minded about home learning. If you cannot work with your local district, your homeschool network can suggest options available to you. Your network is your safety net. Do not be intimidated by what seems to be a preponderance of rules and regulations. As with anything new, it seems to be overwhelming. Once reading and research has been accomplished, you know what needs to be done and it is the same year after year. You develop a working structure and with it comes confidence and comfort. All the information-gathering pays off and any problems encountered are more manageable than the unhappiness imposed by school.

There is no set way to homeschool and there is no set curriculum other than the one you and your child feel meets your family's needs. Learning about the multitude of programs available, homeschooling support groups, area resources and, most of all, your rights as a homeschooling family will enable you to bring learning, direction and some peace into the life of your Asperger's child.

CHAPTER SIX

Practical Tips

Parents home educating an AS child find out what works and what doesn't as far as presenting material and encouraging productivity. Each situation is unique and every family will have its own way of doing things, but soon an operating style emerges and wonderful things start happening. There are some tried and true strategies parents have used that help create productive learning environments for AS homeschoolers. A few of them are mentioned here.

Celia discovered that there would be days when James would accomplish absolutely nothing. Usually these days occurred when he was particularly bothered by something and the perseveration typical of AS had a strong hold on him. Ultimately he would work his way out of such a down day. Other days would just be "off" for whatever reason. When she first started educating James, Celia was preoccupied with getting him to produce a high volume of work each and every day. This was not realistic. She would get frustrated and nag him. Celia's prodding was a waste of time and caused friction between mother and son. Lorraine, James' former third grade teacher, came up with a successful plan for such down times.

Well in advance of starting new lessons, Celia would review the materials. She would find out what was coming up in science, history, English, etc. Before presenting the work, Celia would procure videotapes or audiotapes that supported the curriculum. For example, James was always involved in an English course that required novels to be read. Through her local bookstore (where she was able to get a home educator's discount card) she ordered books on tape for all of the novels. She kept these on hand. If James was having a low performance day she would have him work on a novel by listening to one of the audio series. He enjoyed this very much and it made many of the harder books more palatable. It didn't matter if the novel was supposed to be presented at a later time in the course work. What was important was that James was getting the story, enjoying the literature and getting something positive done on a day that would otherwise be sluggish.

Similarly videotapes would come in handy. When American history was being studied Celia obtained the Ken Burns PBS series on the Civil War. Sister Wendy's PBS art series was available when art history was being covered. These tapes, and many others like them, were invaluable to James and Celia. Whenever there was an off day, Celia was prepared to have James presented with enriching information. The videos were not always specific to courses like the

books on tape for the novels, but James was learning from
them.

Of course, these tapes were expensive, but Celia's
bookstore had a buy back program. Sometimes she would
turn tapes in toward new purchases, but most of the time
James wanted to keep the tapes for his own collection. He
became enthralled with a *David Copperfield* audio series. He
listened to it often and thoroughly enjoyed the complicated tale. Celia chose to purchase audiotapes and videotapes, but often families use the video section of their local
libraries where many of the PBS series and other educational films are available.

Thanks to a suggestion from John, Celia made her own
books on tape. James was an excellent reader, but it was
hard for him to focus on texts if the subject was not of particular interest to him. Sometimes his required reading
went very slowly and Celia felt as if the work would never
get done. This was frustrating to her. She bought a small,
handheld, inexpensive dictating unit and some blank tapes.
Celia had to read ahead in the textbooks to know what was
coming up. Rather than read ahead silently, she read out
loud into the recorder. She would mark each tape according to subject and chapter. A basket was kept on the dining
room table with the tapes neatly organized in it. When
James was ready for the next tape he would just go and get
the one he needed.

Dictating chapters provided some healthy distance
between mother and son. Along with reading from the
texts, Celia would provide direction about illustrations,
graphs and maps. This allowed her to direct James without
hovering around him. It gave him a greater sense of inde-

pendence and lessened the level of intensity that can come with homeschooling. Whenever she drove James to his math, art or swim lessons, Celia would bring a tote bag with the materials necessary to dictate. She would get a coffee and find a quiet spot, oftentimes the car, where she could get the work done. Sometimes the dictating was an effort, but James enjoyed working from the tapes and following along in the textbooks.

Many families have found that creating his own schedule can be very empowering for the Asperger's student. After being at school where everyone is told where to be and what to do at all times, the new homeschooler feels secure when he can have some control over his day. Each day brings obligations and commitments and by maintaining his own daily calendar and weekly schedule, the student learns time management, responsibility and goal setting. James created his own schedule and posted it in his room. He also had a calendar with large squares so he could keep track of daily appointments. Adjustments needed to be made from time to time, but James felt less unnerved by change when he had some input into how it would be managed.

Keeping a journal has been useful for some AS homeschoolers. James and Celia started keeping a notebook where they would write messages back and forth. Sometimes they would get on each other's nerves as the lessons went on day after day. In an effort to keep tensions to a minimum, they decided to write notes about whatever issue was causing problems. They could say what needed to be said and resolve it without having any arguments. This tactic was so successful that James would write journal notes to both his father and mother about all sorts of subjects. Oftentimes he would have questions that would be awkward for a teen to discuss with his parents. These topics could be broached through the journal. He would simply leave the journal in a designated spot. When Celia or John saw it there, they would read the entry, respond, and put the journal back in the same location for James to pick up his answer. A few parents have said that this journal suggestion was attempted and their AS teen was not responsive to it at all. It did work well for James, however, and his writing skills improved as he tried to present his ideas clearly. Eventually James seemed to become too dependent on the journal, and after a few years it was discontinued.

Reading out loud is a favorite thing to do for many homeschooling families. Celia and James enjoyed getting comfortable on the couch with some snacks and reading short stories. This became particularly enjoyable when James got into the works of Edgar Allan Poe. What started out as a technique to assist James through some rather difficult reading, became a family tradition. Not a Halloween season goes by without a Poe story being shared by the family. This approach was also used when audiotapes were not available for a particular novel. Often the wording in older prose was very confusing to James. By reading out loud, the story could be halted at any time so that expressions or words he didn't understand could be explained.

Asperger's students have difficulty writing essays or papers because they don't always have the organizational skills to pull needed information together. When a paper had to be done or a test essay needed to be sent to the correspondence school, James would make up index cards with pertinent information. He then would organize these cards according to the points he wanted to convey. He would sit and look at the cards, formulate his sentences out loud and Celia would type them on the computer. Soon a coherent structure would develop and the writing assignment would be complete.

As the years went by, James mastered this technique and eventually didn't need assistance. If a very large paper had to be done and he was feeling overwhelmed, his mother would again take on the role of secretary. When such assignments are necessary it can be helpful to allow the student to dictate with someone else doing the typing. Although James and others with AS are usually quite good on the computer, lengthy typing can be a distraction when juggling a lot of information.

Rather than hovering over their student, parents have found Post-it notes to be helpful. In an effort to help her son organize his thoughts for writing assignments, one mother would have him write down important points on Post-its. She would then stick them around the computer screen. He would remove each one as the point was incorporated into the writing assignment. Post-it notes are great reminders to place on the front of texts to indicate assignments. The same mother used Post-its throughout texts to make important points about what her son was reading. They allowed her to say what she needed to without being right with her son.

Although approaches to home education vary, quite a few parents of Asperger's children choose to use purchased curriculums. There is a wide variety available to the consumer and it is important to look carefully before you buy one. If you are looking for a high school curriculum, be aware that many programs require that a certified teacher acts as a proctor during testing. This can be a hassle to the homeschooling parent who would have to make arrangements for the proctor to either come to the home or else take the student to the proctor. Look for a program that does not require proctored testing.

An added feature is if the curriculum allows open book testing. The philosophy behind open book testing is that the student learns how to handle texts and locate material. Learning becomes more pleasurable with the stress of timed, proctored testing removed. Celia and James utilized such a program. It was very structured and demanding, but not a problem because of the testing policy. The program was fully accredited. There are AS students who have gone with curriculums that are not accredited because the material and testing format suited their needs. It is important to go with what works for your individual student. What matters is that your child is learning and his Asperger's style is being accommodated, not the credentials of the correspondence school.

Some programs require foreign language study and others do not. In any event, it is wonderful to expose your child to other languages and cultures. One family was using a well-known nonaccredited program that suited their student's needs. There was no language requirement. Concerned that her son was missing out on an important aspect of his education, the mother approached a retired Latin teacher who lived down the street. The teacher was thrilled to take the AS student for lessons a couple of times a week.

The boy loved Latin, learned a tremendous amount and developed a friendship with an older person. In addition, the lessons provided some extra income for the retired teacher. This arrangement stayed in place for years. Another family had their AS homeschooler take French lessons from the mother of a young girl with Asperger's. The mother had majored in French and was a certified teacher. The situation was ideal as the teacher was well versed in AS as well as French.

Resources are available if you just look for them. Whether it be a retired teacher on your street, another parent you know, your local homeschool group, arts center, or nearby college, opportunities are plentiful for the homeschooling family. If you live near a college or university it can be helpful to post an ad with a particular department. For example, if your AS student is anxious to study physics and this just isn't your realm, you can advertise with the physics department of a college near you.

Many college students want and need to earn extra money tutoring. You must interview the student, however, and confirm that he or she understands the basics about Asperger's. If you are not sure about the potential tutor, skip it and hold off until you find someone you are comfortable with. Make it clear that the engagement is not short-term. Once you undertake a line of study, you want to stay with it and not be subject to the whims of a college student who may tire of a tutoring job.

Parents who engage college tutors find it helpful to bring the AS student to the college or university for the lesson. This gets the homeschooler out into an interesting environment with opportunities for meeting and seeing all types of people. It also makes the job possible for a tutor who may have transportation issues. By bringing the student to the tutor you are broadening your chances of finding someone helpful to your child. Not all college students have cars and can come to your home. Also, you time a lesson so it is convenient for your tutor who may have a complicated class schedule. These efforts are all worth it if you link up with someone your AS student likes. By making the logistics easier for your tutor, you make it possible for a relationship to continue for a long time. It will only benefit your homeschooling efforts.

Teaching self-help skills is critical for the Asperger's young person. When a family is homeschooling, more time is available to learn about laundry, cooking, cleaning and other everyday necessities. It is helpful to schedule time each week to focus in on one of these skills. If the task is built into a schedule, then there is a greater chance for success, rather than just waiting for an opportunity to present itself.

James became particularly good at grocery shopping. Celia would give him a set amount of money and a list of things to buy. They would go to the market together, but separate within the store. James would have to keep track of how much he was spending to make sure he had enough money when he got to the register. Celia would keep a general eye on things without James knowing so that if any problems arose at the check-out she could intervene. James enjoyed these excursions. They made him feel as though he was really growing toward independence. It also gave him a good sense of just how much things cost.

James' final year of homeschooling brought with it a math choice. He could continue with a very advanced math, or sign up for a personal math course. James and his parents decided on the personal math course. This involved learning about a checking account, types of bank accounts, taxes, insurance, credit cards, and the many everyday math encounters we all have. As the course progressed, James was taught some financial skills in stages. For example, when checking accounts were covered, Celia and John opened one for him. The same with credit cards. He was given a credit card with a very low limit. He learned how to use it in a store and how to pay the bill when it was received. Using the card he learned to order clothing from a catalog store which specialized in the comfortable styles he liked. Acquiring these skills under the direct supervision of his parents and the math tutor gave James a feeling of confidence and responsibility.

There are always a few areas where the homeschooling parent lacks skills. Celia was definitely not athletic. As he got older James tired of his therapeutic swim classes and wanted to try new sports. His father stepped in to assist Celia with this aspect of his son's education. John's active participation gave Celia much needed breaks and provided an opportunity for father and son to enjoy some special times together. John was an expert skier. Since they lived in northern New England, excellent ski areas were within easy driving distance of home. James received one-on-one ski instruction from his father. He became good at it and enjoyed cross-country as well as downhill. Precautions were taken, such as the use of a head helmet. Also, small walkie-talkies were carried so communication could be maintained if they got separated.

Opportunities arose where John and James were able to participate in group outings to various ski facilities. These were sponsored by a neighbor's company and gave James a chance to go on excursions where he felt welcomed and comfortable. This situation was very different from the middle school field trips where long bus rides were an invitation for teasing and torment. It was noted that on one ski excursion James got confused about social expectations. About seven people, including James, had all been sitting on the bus together and stayed together as they took the lift to a chosen trail. Once at the top everyone started skiing down, each at his or her own pace. James thought that they were all supposed to continue staying together and ski as a pack. This deviation from what he expected to happen upset him. John explained the social dynamics of engaging in a solo sport, yet being part of a group. The problem did not repeat itself.

John and James explored other activities together. They joined a state-wide cycling club that sponsored group excursions. Sometimes they would hike by themselves or be included in a group with family friends. James' enthusiasm for these sports would wax and wane. He required several days' notification before an activity was to take place. Sometimes John wanted to take advantage of particularly fine skiing or cycling conditions. There would also be occasional last-minute invitations to participate in group hikes. James would not go unless he had received the proper notification. This was frustrating for his parents because so many decisions about such activities are made on the spur of the moment.

Eventually James realized that he was missing out on some good times by adhering to his notification rules. His desire to be more social eventually overrode his need for advanced notice and he became cooperative about last-minute opportunities. Certainly not a candidate for local gyms, James was also able to learn some basic weight-lifting techniques from a family friend. Lifting a set amount of weights every morning continues to be an integral part of his daily schedule.

Sport activities, trips, visits to museums, theaters and local outings are all part of your child's education. Maintain a record of them for the portfolio evaluation. Keep ticket stubs, brochures or handouts from places you and your child have been. Write the date on them to refresh your memory later on. Have a separate enrichment box with your yearly homeschool materials. Toss the brochures or ticket items into the box. It is helpful to keep a disposable camera in the car. Whenever you do anything of an enriching nature, even if it is just stopping at a roadside historical marker, take a quick photo of your child there. When the photo is developed, date it and toss it into the enrichment box. It is proof that you are providing a positive educational environment.

In addition to the enrichment box, Celia kept an ongoing notebook. She noted whenever James was involved in any type of educational activity other than his curriculum studies. She included shows on PBS or any of the video series purchased for him. When the time came for the portfolio review, all activities were listed in chronological order. The items in the box supported her listing. The certified teacher who conducted the review never checked the box, but did always look at Celia's listing. It is not necessary to report extra activities performed with your homeschooler, but it is wise to keep a record of them for your own purposes. You may currently have a good relationship with your superintendent or participating agent. Personnel changes, however, and the next person taking over that position may not be quite as open-minded about homeschooling. By maintaining a record of your enriching activities you have further documentation of your work.

Always keep your materials. At the end of each year simply box up what you are done with. Mark the box according to grade and store it in an accessible but out-of-the-way place such as the attic. Just as in keeping a record of extra activities, you want to maintain yearly records in case your home education is ever called into question. Never dispose of an evaluation as this is proof of your child's education. Most families never have problems with their districts, but you have to maintain records as if that might happen. You will probably never be questioned, but it is a good idea to have everything handy, just in case. It is part of approaching home education intelligently. Your homeschooling support groups can provide excellent tips on record-keeping.

CHAPTER SEVEN

Burnout

The burnout experienced by parents who homeschool Asperger's children is real and can never be minimized. Living day to day with an AS person is very demanding, both intellectually and emotionally. Add to that the responsibilities of home education and you have a daunting task. Knowing that burnout will show itself periodically, and having a plan in place to deal with it, is essential.

Some parents dealing with Asperger's fear home education because they think the stress burden would be too much to handle. They worry about the demands and intensity of spending so much time with their child. There is definitely stress when homeschooling any child, never mind one with very special needs. It is a tall order and a tremendous undertaking. Self-maintenance is crucial.

The good news is that most families who homeschool say that they would never go back to the old days of dealing with the educational system. The pressures of meeting a child's educational needs at home are nothing like the pressures of fighting for that child's very survival within a nonaccepting bureaucracy. As one mother of a young Asperger's girl states:

> Some days I'm very burned out, but I always somehow regroup. There is less stress in our lives and fewer outbursts. We will never go back. She has started learning for the first time. School was all struggle, no academic gains. I enjoy home-schooling and will probably miss it one day.

Everyone handles demands differently with individual levels of tolerance. We each have our own survival techniques that help us manage difficult situations. Know what works to calm yourself and implement it so you can help your child. Being the parent of an Asperger's child is like being a passenger on an airplane. If there is a change in pressure, the oxygen masks are released. The flight crew gives instructions to place the mask over your own face and get yourself stabilized before you assist the child sitting next to you. You are of no service to anyone if you are not in good shape yourself. Obviously when a problem moment arises for your AS child you can't jet off to Tahiti to relax and regroup (no matter how much you would like to), but you can make adjustments to your everyday life that will help you and, in turn, help your child. Of course, this is easier said than done.

Once the constant peer comparisons of school are eliminated, parents report a feeling of true appreciation for their child. Pressure can still be felt, however, from the unwanted and unsolicited input of others. Such insidious pressure can interfere with the pleasure of home educating and contribute to self-doubt. It can have a subtle effect over time and contribute to burnout as the homeschooling parents feel the need to defend their choices to the universe.

An unfortunate example of this influence was the mother of a third grade girl with AS. She spoke up at a recent workshop for parents considering home education for AS children. She said that her daughter was having a terrible time in school. In her heart this mother felt that homeschooling would be the best thing for her daughter and herself. The problem was her relatives. Every time the subject of homeschooling came up they let their opinions be known about how awful it was to remove children from the socialization of school. Interestingly, none of them knew anyone who actually did homeschool. The young mother was torn. She was so intimidated by their views that she was unable to address her daughter's needs as well as her own.

Although this woman had not started homeschooling, her problem with unsolicited advice reflects a common situation. It is an issue known to all Asperger's families. Unwanted comments cause pain and confusion to the recipient. It is essential that parents homeschooling an AS student keep people who so freely offer opinions at arm's length. Creating boundaries for yourself and your child prevents negative influences from seeping into your environment.

Celia painfully discovered that just because someone was a relative didn't mean that they understood, or were sympathetic toward, her situation. The same was true for long-time friends. She and John took a long, hard look at the people in their world and decided that armchair experts served no useful purpose. John and Celia were not unkind people, but self-preservation demanded a weeding out of tension sources. Invitations were politely declined. Questions about James and his education were answered pleasantly with little information. Gradually the boundaries were established. Celia recalls:

> I know I've hurt some feelings along the way, but the most important thing is our little family and our tranquility. Old friends who were critical of our decision were not helping me. They were making me feel stressed out because I thought I had to defend my position to them. Finally I decided that the only thing that mattered was James and his success. If friends or relatives were causing me to stress, I just didn't include them in my life. Sometimes this was very hard, but it had to be done.

Included in these efforts to create functional boundaries were other parents of Asperger's children. Celia found that the AS and homeschool network she had created was a lifeline for her and essential to homeschooling success. Some parents, however, go beyond being supportive to actually being a drain. Celia encountered a few people like this. They wanted her to have all the answers pertaining to their own AS children. In an effort to be kind, Celia gave some of these parents a great deal of her time. She found that they took the focus away from the task at hand, which was her child, his AS issues, and education. Celia learned the hard way that a drain of her psychic energy did not help her family. Networking is crucial and a great boost, but a careful eye has to be kept on the boundaries. One way to burn yourself out is to give so much of yourself away that there is nothing left for you. John states, "This is not about hurt feelings, this is about survival. Keep the world at arm's length." If you feel stress, it is a warning sign that all is not well. Identify the source and enact a plan of action.

Once you have made your decision to homeschool, it is a waste of valuable energy to engage in second guessing. Of course, you will wonder at first if you made the right choice, but no matter what you do it will be better for your child than an unhappy school setting. You do not have to defend your beliefs or choices to anyone. If someone disagrees with you, that is their right. If you fight the battle against the world, you will exhaust yourself. A mother of a homeschooled Asperger's teen states:

> I think our life together is like an onion. To get to the core, you have to peel off layer after layer. That's how I think of the people and things in our life that stress us. I just have to keep peeling away until I get to the essential core. That is the part that really counts.

Support groups of one type or another are crucial in preventing burnout. Families living in remote areas depend heavily on the support they receive from Asperger's and homeschool websites. Just knowing that others appreciate what is being experienced in your own household limits feelings of isolation. Some parents attend monthly groups while others reach out only when necessary. The point is to have your network in place so when you feel headed for a slump you can bolster yourself with positive input.

Quite often homeschooling problems stem from unrealistic expectations. Parents who are products of an educational system have a hard time breaking away from their own experience of a set amount of work to be done daily. In home education progress is not measured by the output of worksheets and it is sometimes hard to know what your child is accomplishing. Celia noticed that there were days when James just didn't seem to be absorbing much of anything. This would be especially bothersome to her if important unit materials were being presented. He would sometimes surprise her weeks later by talking about the information she thought he had missed. She would be amazed to discover that he had been listening and learning after all. Leave your daily expectations behind. If not, you will wear yourself out wondering and worrying.

The more responsibility you gradually give to your child, the more you can step back from your homeschooling tasks. Younger AS children who are being home educated are often not receptive to accepting responsibilities. Many would make a decision to do nothing but play computer games. Others take great pride working independently. The introduction of cleaning up, shopping, cooking and other self-help skills eventually pays off with a more self-sufficient teen. Just knowing that you are working toward independence is a great motivator for everyone involved. Activities outside the home are also important as they provide periodic breaks from each other. Time away from your student provides a mental break for you both.

It is impossible to impart to your AS student every bit of factual information available in the universe. What is possible is to think of oneself, not as a teacher, but as an educational facilitator. Parents act as facilitators when they try to obtain the right diagnosis and services. Once the facilitating mind-set is established for educational purposes, a lot of unnecessary pressure is lifted. This approach is especially helpful for those Asperger's children who resist direct teaching. By providing access to information, the parent is setting the stage for learning in a happy, self-directed setting.

Contacting support groups, early morning quiet times, scented candles, watching favorite videos, praying, meditating, and leisurely baths when time permits are just a few of many suggestions from parents to help control burnout. What is evident is that keeping yourself grounded is of the utmost importance. Don't deny yourself the little things that keep you going. Celia would spend extra money every week buying her favorite brand of Irish tea. It may not sound significant, but she enjoyed that brand and it brought her some comfort during trying times. The little comforts can add up and help you get through what needs to be done. One parent says, "AS is like ocean waves. I never feel in control, but I do at least feel like we can surf through it." Recognize what you need to keep you afloat, no matter how minor, and incorporate it into your life.

CHAPTER EIGHT

Stories and Reflections

The decision to withdraw an Asperger's child from school and start home education does not have to be a scary one. Input from parents who have already been through the process can be very helpful. Just knowing that others have confronted the change and used homeschooling to bring a better life to their children is a great gift. Every family and situation is different, yet there are few regrets associated with homeschooling. The influence of this choice on the people involved is remarkable.

James is now a very successful student at an art college located about thirty miles from home. He has his own car and commutes daily. His social life revolves around art and he particularly enjoys attending the shows of local artists. As he meets more and more people with similar interests, James' world broadens, his social skills improve and he develops more self-esteem. His future looks very bright. Celia reflects:

> I never wanted to be in the position of saying, "If only I had…" I truly believe that if we had left James in the middle school and had him proceed onto the local high school he would have been destroyed. There is no other way to say it. By homeschooling James we saved him from serious emotional and psychological harm. My husband and I not only saved him, we saved ourselves because our lives would have been very sad. When I look at him now and see the fine young man he is, I am so incredibly proud.

When asked about the past, Celia says:

> All my life I always did everything that was expected of me. I was an obedient child and followed every rule. I hated school, but I did all that was expected and more. This time it was different. This was about my son. He is the most important thing in the world to my husband and me. I knew that he would be badly damaged after years in the system. No one was going to dominate me anymore. My son's life was at stake. I have never regretted my decision to withdraw him from school for a moment. Homeschooling made me look at the entire world differently. I am stronger. I look back and see how easily controlled I was through most of my life. Homeschooling defined me and made my son. Not only did it give my son his life, it gave me mine. It taught me to be an independent person and gave my son a very real chance to be who he is today.

A single mother, Pam started homeschooling her Asperger's daughter after the little girl spent only six weeks in first grade. Meghan had attended a special ed preschool and was assigned an aide to assist her through regular kindergarten and first grade. She exhibited the usual difficulties of an AS child in a school setting. There were sensory integration issues and the class size was hard for her to handle. She couldn't do circle time, had trouble with transitions and resisted being told what to do. Pam felt that a good IEP was in place, yet things were not going well for her daughter.

When she was in kindergarten, Meghan learned to think of herself as "trouble" and began calling herself a "loser." Behavior problems outside of school started to erupt. These activities continued into first grade. Meghan's pediatrician kept telling Pam to keep her child in the school setting until she learned to adjust. Pam followed the advice of both the IEP team and pediatrician. She remembers:

> There were many meltdowns. They happened getting ready to go to school, during school and when I picked her up. I knew she was miserable. I couldn't sleep. I worried all the time.

It took hours to calm Meghan down at the end of the school day and then fears about the next day would start to build.

Pam felt that the IEP team did not take Meghan's situation seriously. It also did not place an emphasis on outside evaluations. Team members claimed to understand AS and sensory issues but did not show it in their daily actions.

The teachers and aides were not properly trained in AS and SI. The environment was too busy and Meghan was seen as a behavior problem rather than someone with a neurological problem. Rather than learn more information and get more training, the teachers and aides became angry with her. She didn't understand them and they didn't understand her. We fought hard for a good IEP, but no one at the school would implement it. We needed a solution!

In an effort to control Meghan's outbursts, the school would sometimes restrain her. Pam learned about this after it had already occurred several times. At one point the first grade aide became so exasperated with Meghan's noncompliant behavior that she angrily put her hands on the child. Meghan was so traumatized that she broke out in hives. Pam filed a complaint and the aide was eventually fired. After two plus years of team meetings, school was a hopeless situation. The final straw came when Meghan talked of suicide because of the stress at school. The little girl with AS wanted to end her life at age seven.

Pam removed her daughter from school and began home education. Meghan had a strong need to choose her own agenda and Pam went with her daughter's choices. She continues with this approach saying:

I interject with math and handwriting and Meghan guides the rest. She goes to the library and chooses what appeals to her. We do activities and field trips based on her current interest.

Meghan has many varied interests such as smoke detectors, mermaids and ocean creatures, fairies and flying, anatomy, simple machines and building toys. She dictates imagined stories to her mother and together they make them into books. Her father helps with her interest in mechanical things and does aquatherapy with her. Occupational therapy and speech services are still available to her through the school district. She also has private OT sessions. Pam recalls:

> She was so active and resistant in school because they didn't know how to deal with her. They made little attempt to teach her. She didn't start doing grade-level work until we started homeschooling. Dealing with how Meghan felt while she was at school was horrible. I wish I took her out two years sooner.

According to her mother, Meghan is now more centered and has much more respect for herself and her abilities. There are still some residual behaviors and her family feels that she continues to feel wounded by her school experience.

> I don't know how else she could be educated at this point. She has strict areas of interest. She needs to control and be in charge of her learning. If she is allowed to proceed using these traits as gifts, she flourishes. If these traits are denied she gets angry, scared, defeated and threatens self-harm. She needs a mentor one on one and homeschooling is our way of providing that. Meghan's social skills training is also more effective now since the overload of interaction at school

has been eliminated. She spends time with people of varying ages. I don't think she needs peer socialization as much as it's offered in the school environment. She has her OT, speech, swimming and library activities outside of the home.

Pam makes some important points in her story. She listened to the input of others until it became obvious that her daughter's self-esteem was being seriously eroded. A bad foundation was being established and nothing positive could come from it. Meghan and Pam feel that they finally have control over their lives. Pam comments:

> The decision to homeschool has created financial difficulty, but we are stronger and happier. It has helped my relationship with my daughter. I feel like I have a purpose and that I'm doing the best I can for my child.

Like Celia many years before, Pam sensed a point of no return was being approached and acted upon it.

Kate homeschools her nine-year-old son, Tim, along with his siblings. Tim is diagnosed with Asperger's Syndrome. He has never attended school. A certified teacher, Kate had always planned on homeschooling her children. She says:

> This decision was reinforced by Tim's high needs and intensity from birth, his obvious giftedness and the realization when he was turning five that he absolutely would not fit in a regular classroom. My initial decision was based on my belief that children can obtain a better, broader, richer, more individualized, more child-led, and less stressful

education at home. I can't even imagine what Tim's life would be like if he had to be in a classroom every day. In fact, I am quite certain that he would be suicidal already.

Over the years Kate has taught for a small homeschool co-op group and Tim has occasionally participated in her courses. Even with his mother as the teacher, he has not comfortably engaged in class activity, rather learning the material at home in his own time. Kate currently uses a purchased curriculum that she adapts to suit her son's needs. "Although I plan a lot and use a curriculum, I have seldom found a concept to teach that he hasn't already figured out for himself," she says.

Tim participates in a wide variety of activities such as karate, swimming, music lessons, scouting, a speech therapy group and a gifted class that his mother teaches for the school system. Such activities provide opportunities for positive socialization. She explains:

We try to have an activity outside the house almost every day. We talk regularly about social skills and plan skills he can practice away from home. Thirty kids in a class quietly doing math pages while my son ping pongs off the walls is not socializing.

Homeschooling her Asperger's son gives Kate the chance to spend as much time as she can working with him. She believes that, if her son were in school, too much of her energy would be spent dealing with the school system itself. When asked if she felt that homeschooling was generally more beneficial to the Asperger's child, Kate made the following comment:

> Absolutely. Homeschooling is much better adapted to their needs socially, sensorially and academically. I think all kids would do better with more individualized education, but our kids rarely fit the programs planned for mass education.

It isn't always easy for Kate.

> I never feel like I have time for myself but, God willing, life is long and childhood is short. A lot of problems come from what you expect. I don't expect my days to be easy right now, though I hope the day will come when they are easier. This is just where I am and it's hard to see where I would otherwise be. I would not put my children in school unless I had to become the sole support for my family and there was no one else to take on the teaching.

Kate feels that she may eventually continue with her classroom teaching career, but right now she is committed to teaching her children in their own home.

Lynn is an engaging young woman with AS presently in her early twenties. She is obviously highly intelligent and has always been a good student. Her mother, Anne, removed her from high school during sophomore year. Lynn was age seventeen as a sophomore since she had spent two years in kindergarten as well as first grade. Throughout the years of public school an annual IEP was developed and aides were occasionally supplied.

During her daughter's time in elementary school, Anne had trouble getting the IEP enforced.

> Over the years we were continually fighting the
> battle to get things to work. The speech and
> language therapist and the occupational therapist
> were great, but classroom teachers hardly imple-
> mented what had been discussed. In spite of this, I
> always felt that we would eventually mold school
> to be what it needed to be for Lynn.

Although she had some obvious social limitations, Lynn
functioned as a member of her school community and
achieved good grades.

Academics were not a problem as Lynn progressed
through junior high, but she did find the school environment extremely hectic and confusing. What did become
evident, however, was that she was becoming more and
more socially isolated. Many of Lynn's Asperger's traits
which were tolerated in the elementary years were now
being noticed by unkind teens. Her lack of eye contact, rit-
ualistic behaviors and misinterpretation of social cues made
her an easy target for teasing.

A quiet, polite person, Lynn recalls her junior high
days:

> The social stuff definitely got harder. It really wore
> me down. I think I was picked on because of my
> innocence. They made fun of my clothes. They'd
> prod and wait for the reaction. When I went on
> field trips no one wanted to sit with me. The
> message I got was that I was bad.

Lynn stuck with school because teachers kept reassuring
her that everything would get better in high school.

The two years that Lynn spent in high school were very traumatic, not only for her, but for Anne. Again, academics were not the issue as Lynn continued to be a conscientious student. The pattern of social dynamics that had been established in junior high not only continued into high school, but escalated. Lynn poignantly shares her memories:

> People just stayed away from me. They ignored me mostly. I wasn't able to tolerate the confusion of the cafeteria so I just walked the hallways during lunch because I didn't know where to go. There were students who constantly tormented me. It wore me down. I felt like a warrior every day. I pretended I was a warrior going into battle. That helped me get through it. I felt like I was drowning.

Lynn's daily struggles centered around very simple things. An example is a lesson from a social skills therapy session at school. She was taught to smile at fellow students in an attempt to appear friendly. When Lynn tried to implement what she learned, the other students noticed that she was smiling a lot and made fun of her. Lynn claims, "They just wouldn't let me be. I would start crying in school because of year after year of stress build-up. I actually felt sick from stress."

Anne remembers this period of time as being unbearably difficult.

> Everything in the high school culture was centered around being cool. You pick on others so others won't pick on you. It's not always the

school system that's the problem, but the culture
of school. You must be cool.

Lynn perseverated a great deal about what happened to her
during the day and Anne would spend tremendous
amounts of time helping her cope with hurt feelings. The
memories of past insults seemed as fresh in Lynn's mind as
the day they happened. Then she would encounter new
ones with each school day. "If not for being picked on, we
would have stuck it out," recalls Anne, "but I just couldn't
take it anymore."

Lynn is a talented artist. During high school she began
drawing pictures to express how she felt about her experiences. She created a pastel drawing of a very beautiful
lavender flower with thin, wavy red lines emerging from it
and running down to the bottom of the paper. When
showing the picture today, Lynn gently explains that the
flower represented her and the red lines represented her
life's blood. She felt that her very life force was gradually
being drained from her because of the social environment
she had to endure daily.

Anne remembers the day she made the decision to
remove Lynn from school.

> I will never forget it. It was January and we were
> vacationing when it hit me. I felt that we had her in
> school and it was like someone trying to live on
> another planet. You have a suit and you get your
> oxygen brought in. We were working to get her to
> survive in a totally foreign atmosphere. I didn't
> know anyone who homeschooled, but I had read a
> lot of articles. I felt badly that Lynn never had time
> to spend on what she was interested in. We had

spent too much time on her weaknesses, not on her strengths.

I had to talk Lynn into it. Even though the situation at school was bad, the idea of change was scary to her. I couldn't figure out why she wouldn't just jump out of the cage she was in. I think she was so shell-shocked that she couldn't see freedom when it came. When I pulled her out the teachers never looked at the positives of homeschooling, only the negatives. They were very upset with me and questioned what kind of life Lynn would have. They felt it would be too closed. I felt a sense of great relief, but also fear. It was like being on a trip. We didn't know where we were going and we were going it alone.

It took a period of time for Lynn to become acclimated to homeschooling. During the transition, Anne saw some repetitive behaviors such as playing cassettes back and forth. These behaviors eventually became less pronounced. Lynn states:

When I first began homeschooling I did a lot of reading to try and understand why people do what they do. It took me a long time to get over how I felt and how I was not treated well.

Once the transitional time passed, Lynn enthusiastically explored her favorite subjects. No set curriculum was used. She would go to the library of a nearby university and select books centered around her interests which were art, architecture, Chinese culture, and political propaganda.

After leaving school, Lynn created a beautiful pastel drawing of an angel with magnificent wings of varying colors. She says that the angel and its wings represent the freedom she felt once she was away from the unkindness of her classmates. The wings of the angel are in stark contrast to Lynn's prior drawing of the lavender flower losing its life's blood.

> I didn't know myself then, I've healed to a certain extent. Just to discover who I am has been healing. If I had stayed in school there would have been a lot more damage. I still have struggles, but I've learned to listen to myself and be confident with who I am and what my limits are.

Lynn is currently continuing her independent studies. She is learning all she can about AS and her goal is to somehow become an advocate for those with Asperger's Syndrome.

Thinking back on her homeschooling time, Anne says:

> I felt empowered because I finally had control. Lynn had a lot of intellectual interests we could focus on. I still feel badly that we couldn't make the school system work.

Her only real regret is that she didn't impose more structure onto Lynn's day when they first began home education. Specifically, she wishes that she had allotted time to teach self-help skills. "AS people need structure," she says. "I wish I had put more emphasis on that."

What is right for some families is not right for others. Sharon, a career special education teacher, tried homeschooling her daughter and Asperger's son. After a couple of months, she found it too limiting to be around home and children so much. An extremely active person, Sharon found it hard to organize their days without the routine of school. The children enjoyed learning at home, but Sharon found she just couldn't get organized unless she had deadlines imposed by an outside source. She put the children back in school and returned to her job. Although home education was not appropriate for her family, she says she is glad that they at least tried it. She always would have wondered if she had made a mistake by not giving it a chance. She has no regrets and believes that public school is the setting that works for both her son and herself.

Another mother states:

> Homeschooling is not always perfect. It is demanding and a lot of patience is needed. You get a double whammy of homeschooling needs and Asperger's needs, but the rewards are tremendous. Your child can actually live and you can see who your child really is, not what a system is trying to create out of a cookie cutter.

Make your choice based on the best you can personally do for your Asperger's child. Don't let advocates of either public schools or home education make you feel guilty about the educational choices you have made. We all do the best we can based on individual circumstances.

People have commented that it takes a lot of courage to homeschool any child, never mind one with AS. That may be true, but if a child is learning a minimal amount, suffering from unkindness and accepting it all because that is the signal he receives from his parents, then he will not strive for anything better in life. By having your child tolerate an unsatisfactory educational and social environment, you show that this is what you think is best for him. As Lynn astutely comments, "I felt like I was being pushed toward mediocrity." No wonder so many Asperger's students get depressed. How hard it must be to get up each morning and face a setting that pulverizes the essence of who you are in order to make you conform.

There seem to be few regrets mentioned by parents home educating their AS children. One that does emerge, however, is regret at not removing the child from school sooner. Families are often amazed at how long it took them to make their decision. Often mingled with this regret is anger. A child is removed from school for a reason. Usually it is because academic needs are not being met, the social situation is not acceptable, or both. Emotions run high in such circumstances and the parental urge to protect a loved child is in high gear. By the time the student is actually withdrawn from the negative setting, emotions are peaking. It can take some time for feelings to calm down.

Forgotten in the turmoil of the decision-making process are those teachers who have provided help, support and encouragement to the Asperger's student over the years. The last group of teachers encountered is the most vivid in the memories of homeschooling families. It is usually this last unhappy school situation that prompts the decision to home educate. The final impression of school can be very strong.

What needs to be put in perspective is that there are teachers who will never want to understand or be able to accommodate the needs of an Asperger's child. There are others, however, whose talents as educators go beyond the confines of the system in which they operate. Those who are truly called to teach recognize that learning is a very individual experience. Such teachers are like knights on a quest trying desperately to impart knowledge, but also doing battle with a giant bureaucracy that can swallow them up. This type of teacher knows that whether the Asperger's student is in a typical school setting or at home is irrelevant. What does matter is that the child is learning, developing a curiosity for the world around him, and becoming a functional member of the society in which he exists. The ultimate goal is not to debate which approach to education is correct, but finding what will work best for the AS child. When Celia's cousin, Mary, embraced the idea of home education for James by saying, "Why not?", she displayed her ability to think beyond the system she had served for her entire adult life.

Think back over your own life and realize how much you learned outside of school through organizations, museums, mentors, travel, or just reading a good book for pleasure. Don't be overwhelmed by the task of educating your child. It was a greater task to get the Asperger's diagnosis and learn to accept it. Recognize that no one knows, loves or cares about your child the way you do. Others may say they care, but ultimately parents walk a lonely path with their Asperger's child. If the work of others fails, you and your child are left together picking up the pieces of your lives. You are your child's greatest advocate. You know how your child functions and learns better than anyone else. Take strength in that. Many professionals of varying sorts are overconfident. They convey to parents the impression that only professionals have all the answers about what is right for the AS child. No one has all the answers.

You are already your child's teacher and have been from day one. You are probably reteaching what has been presented at school. Every day you are implementing techniques that have proven helpful for young people with AS. It must be remembered, however, that home education is not a fit for every family. Parents should search to find out what the educational opportunities are for their AS child. For those parents who are very concerned about the quality of education and social pressures in today's schools, homeschooling is a legal option that is available to them. Listen to that inner voice. It has guided many parents to seek out better lives for themselves and the Asperger's child they love.

Resources

Must-have books

Dobson, Linda. *The Homeschooling Book of Answers: The 88 Most Important Questions Answered by Homeschooling's Most Respected Voices.* Roseville, CA: Prima Publishing, 1998.

This is an absolute must-have book. There is excellent information on resources, curriculums, state requirements, and a thorough listing of national and statewide homeschool support organizations.

Wade, Theodore E., Jr. (ed) *The Home School Manual: Plans, Pointers, Reasons and Resources.* Bridgman, MI: Gazelle Publications, 1998.

Another reliable source of information with a complete listing of homeschool organizations.

Other important books

Cowlishaw, Kitt and Dowty, Terri. *Home Educating Our Autistic Spectrum Children: Paths Are Made By Walking.* London: Jessica Kingsley Publishers, 2002.

Gatto, John Taylor. *Dumbing Us Down: The Hidden Curriculum of Compulsory Schooling.* Philadelphia, PA: New Society Publishers, 2002.

Check www.johntaylorgatto.com for other books by this inspiring author.

Guterson, David. *Family Matters: Why Homeschooling Makes Sense.* San Diego, CA: Harcourt Brace & Company, 1993.

Farenga, Patrick and Holt, John. *Teach Your Own: The John Holt Book of Homeschooling.* Cambridge, MA: Perseus Publishing, 2003.

A revised edition of a classic book. Excellent ideas, resources, advice and stories.

Magazines

Home Education Magazine

P.O. Box 1083
Tonasket, WA 98855-1083
Phone: ++1(1)800-236-3278 or ++1(1)509-486-1351
E-mail: HEM@home-ed-magazine.com
Website: www.home-ed-magazine.com

This magazine is a good source of encouragement and has many advertisements for curriculums and useful materials. A free resource guide is available.

Homeschooling Consultation Services

Holt Associates, Inc.

P.O. Box 89
Wakefield, MA 01880-5011
Phone: ++1(1)781-395-8508
E-mail: consult@HOLTGWS.com
Website: www.holtgws.com

Questions answered about homeschooling and suggestions made by Susannah Sheffer and Patrick Farenga. Both are highly respected lecturers on homeschooling who follow the educational philosophy of John Holt.